Family Stories from the Attic

Bringing letters and archives alive
through creative nonfiction,
flash narratives, and poetry

Editors
Christi Craig
Lisa Rivero

HIDDEN TIMBER BOOKS
MEANINGFUL BOOKS AND STORIES

MILWAUKEE, WISCONSIN

Hidden Timber Books LLC
5464 N. Port Washington Rd. #C224
Milwaukee, WI 53217

www.hiddentimberbooks.com

Book Layout ©2015 BookDesignTemplates.com

Special discounts are available on quantity purchases by corporations, associations, and others. For details, contact Lisa Rivero, publisher, at the address above.

Family Stories from the Attic/ Christi Craig and Lisa Rivero

1st edition

ISBN 978-0-9906530-4-2 (hardcover)
ISBN 978-0-9906530-8-0 (paperback)

2 3 4 5 6 7 8 9 10

Contents

Preface (Christi Craig) 1

Introduction (Lisa Rivero) 5

Kristine D. Adams 12

   "Wally's World" 13

JoAnne Bennett 20

   "When We Feel Invisible" 21

Aleta Chossek 22

   "A New Life" 23

Sally Cissna 34

   "Come Home, Peter" 35

Gloria DiFulvio 50

   "If She Had Lived" 51

Julia Gimbel 56

   "In a Sailor's Footsteps" 57

Myles Hopper 70

   "Exodus Redux" 71

Margaret Krell 80

   "Tracing My Father's Admonition" 81

Amy Wang Manning 98

   "Extract of Household Registration" 99

Nancy Martin 108

   "The Teetotaler" 109

Patricia Ann McNair 114

   "Climbing the Crooked Trails" 115

Carolou Nelsen 130

   "I Had a Brother" 131

Joanne Nelson 136

   "In My Office" 137

Contents (continued)

Annilee Newton 140

   "Leet" 141

Pam Parker...150

   "The Blue Cardboard Box" 151

Ramona M. Payne 170

   "Without Words" 171

Valerie Reynolds 178

   "She Wrote a Good Letter" 179

Jessica Schnur 182

   "Schnur Family Announcement" 183

Meagan Schultz 188

   "They Were Young Once, Too" 189

Yvonne Stephens 196

   "Syl" 197

   "Letters on Repeat from 728 W Spruce St." 199

Kim Suhr 202

   "Wind the Fabric Tighter" 203

Julie Anne Thorndyke 204

   "Aunt Becker's Secret" 205

About the Editors 207

BY CHRISTI CRAIG

Preface

Explorations, Examinations, and Imaginations

"...every stone on the road precious to me." ~ Stanley Kunitz

It happens on your way home from work. You're stuck in traffic, even though it's barely late afternoon, and a song comes on the radio. Maybe it's George Michael's "Faith," with its toe-tapping beat and instant recall of that MTV video of him in his acid-washed Levis. Maybe it's "a little diddy 'bout Jack and Diane," the summer anthem for you and your best friend when you were seventeen, mostly because it was the song that came on the radio every time the two of you got into the car together. You have always believed in signs.

Your car in the driveway, you toss your bags on the floor as soon as you are inside the house, and you walk upstairs to your daughter's room. A square door grants entry into a small attic space, and there, behind her arrangement of doll accessories and furniture — her own collection of treasures — is a trunk full of yours.

The lock on the chest doesn't hold; the box is brimming with artifacts and antiques, things you carried a thousand miles from where you were born. Fragments from a time before you were a Wisconsinite, before you married and became a mother. Even from

1

a time before you were a writer. Though, sifting through the contents, it's no wonder you turned to the page; the trunk is full of stories.

Under your sorority blanket that marked your identity for the first two years in college, you reach for a terrycloth outfit you wore when you were five or six years old: a pair of shorts and a shirt embroidered with two tiny tennis rackets. You never played tennis, and you left the sorority behind when you fell into your "hippy" years. But it isn't the texture of the wool or the cloth that you admire, it's the faces that appear in your mind with the first sensation of touch. The curly dark hair and broad smile of the first sorority sister to greet you when you pledged—Meredith, from Oklahoma City!—who welcomed you when you had no idea what or where or how to manage the next four years of your life. It's the mellow memories of the time your parents gave you the terrycloth outfit to wear on days when they would take you with them as they played tennis—a tangible reminder of those sunny afternoons basking in the sounds of your parents' laughter.

Beyond the ceramic Holly Hobbie wrapped in tissue paper and a faux-tux costume you wore when you tap-danced and sang "New York, New York" for the fourth-grade talent show, you find what you were looking for: the shoebox of letters. Letters dated 1988, the year you graduated high school and the summer your best friend turned sixteen, the summer when the two of you were supposed to ride the Texas highways together to the mall, the movies, the parking lot parties. You driving your little white hatchback and her in the passenger seat, the windows rolled down and George Michael pouring from the radio, the car filled with the excitement and ambitions of two teenagers on the cusp of life. Instead, you drove her to the airport in June and said a tearful goodbye at the gate as she and her family boarded a plane headed to South Korea for the summer. Worse, for a whole year.

Email was not so popular then, cell phones were for the fancy, and long distance calls ran up the bill dollars a minute, so air mail was your only option. You wrote immediately, scribbling on the tissue-thin paper and titling the first letter "The Day After."

I couldn't help myself. I had to write. I thought I'd wait at least a week or 2, but I saw 3 small Korean boys and thought, I can't stand it any longer.

You wrote almost every day and kept the postman busy in the delivery of envelopes thick with angst, news of changing bodies, nerves (and mothers) as you set off for college. She responded in kind.

Sure your mom is going to cry, you're the last one to leave, it's going to be just her and your dad. She's just being a mom. Don't let it get you down. Speaking of mothers, mine is driving me up the wall. She's complaining now I don't get out and should read books. Those damn books, why does my mom have to be a librarian?

You traded much needed encouragement because, with her overseas and you off to college, you were both in a strange land.

Hey Girlfriend – to the one I love, adore, miss, and so on and so on...

"You're the greatest, and Heather loves me, and that's all I need!" Repeat 3 times a day.

Her words became weekly reminders that distance means nothing where sisters of the heart are concerned.

It was so weird getting your letter about you being sick because right now I can't breathe out of my right nostril; we're even sick together.

Love always. Those letters saved you that summer.

❖ ❖ ❖

Artifacts and antiques become gateways into our past, and we study them as an archeologist might; we sweep aside irrelevant dust, carefully lift the object into the light, and brush fingers across the face of something old to discover something new. Sometimes we put them under lock and key; they are that precious. We may wrap them in soft cotton and tuck them away into the corner of a closet. Inevitably, though, we return to explore them again and again. Such relics never lose their attraction.

Family Stories from the Attic is a collection of explorations: stories, poems, and essays by writers who investigate hand-held pieces of a puzzle — a blue box, a stack of love letters, clippings from the news, pages of a journal, a family registry, and photos. These pages are filled with examinations about a time past, tributes to a person lost or a father-figure remembered. And sometimes these pieces grow from the imagination of the writer. Because in truth, memory is fragile, and we as humans are driven to fill in the gaps. To study every image. To run our finger down every page in a diary, until the words form a link to our history. An answer to our questions. A way to understand our place in the world and our connection to those around us.

And it is in this way that the writing saves us.

Introduction

This anthology has its origins in another time, in secrets and questions, in family stories and a woman who died before I was born.

In the bottom cupboard of an antique sideboard in my grandmother's house were stacks of journals handwritten by her sister, my great-aunt Hattie. Aunt Hattie's name, along with that of her husband, Uncle Bill, had peppered family conversations for as long as I could remember. While I'd never met her, I knew that she was eccentric, beloved but also humored in the way we humor the very young and very old. I knew she was born the eldest of ten children in 1881, married late, lived in Hidden Timber, South Dakota (the inspiration for Hidden Timber Books), and had a brother who had eighteen children (one of whom would go on to have eleven offspring), giving her scores of nieces and nephews and all kinds of once-removed relations. However, she had no children of her own.

At least that's what I thought.

Then, one summer day when I was in high school, my grandmother, who lived on the same farm as my parents and was suffering from shingles at the time, received a letter from a man inquiring about the health history of his grandfather, born in 1911 — to Hattie — and later adopted.

My grandmother's shingles and that letter are paired in my memory, as if her physical pain and the psychological shock became one. It couldn't have been easy for her, then nearly eighty years old, to reconcile the idea of her devout Catholic family with an out-of-wedlock birth. Grandma was twenty-one years younger than Hattie, and by the time the typewritten letter arrived on that hot summer day, all of my grandmother's brothers and sisters and all of their husbands and wives had died. She later learned that other members of the family *had* known about Hattie's child, but Grandma, the baby of the family, was never told, and the topic was not discussed in that era as part of polite conversation.

Grandma was, above all, stoic, so the fact that I even knew about how much she suffered from shingles indicates their severity. Only many years later, after reading Hattie's dairies, did I realize how different Grandma and Hattie were as sisters, like Elinor and Marianne in *Sense and Sensibility*, except the roles were reversed, the elder Hattie's spiritedness in contrast to the younger Louise's seriousness.

Until that summer, my interest in Aunt Hattie's journals had been intermittent. Sometimes I would leaf through them, but the handwriting was difficult to read, and I was daunted by the seventy-seven composition notebooks and ledgers piled high. After learning about the baby she had given up, however, I was drawn more compellingly to secrets that might be in the cupboard. Did the entries contain more information about Hattie's child? Did she ever write about him? Who was this woman who loomed so large in family lore?

So many people, myself included, try to keep diaries. We might write in them during especially trying times or happy times or maybe just because we have nothing else to do. We journal in fits and starts. We begin and then give up.

Not Hattie. She wrote every day, sometimes even rewriting her entries, catching up if she needed to. Only a handful of days are missing from volumes that span from 1920 through 1957.

I began transcribing the entries to share with family members, and she became real to me through her words. Who was Hattie? She loved puzzles and games, especially solitaire, and she and her husband, William, played cards often with neighbors. She recorded scores of local baseball games. She looked forward to getting the mail and reading material. She enjoyed listening to the radio, especially news programs and serials. She butchered hogs on her kitchen table. She didn't like to garden. She tended to be stout and then fat, helped along by her fondness for food and the difficulty she had in physical movement in later years. She was keenly interested in both local and national politics and remembered the anniversary of the death of FDR every year. She seems never to have lost her humor or her sense of wonder and engagement. She was devoted to Will, even when they had rough patches. Both were eccentric and intelligent. He lost his mother and father in the first year of their marriage. She lost her parents within a few years, as well, and they had to make their way on their own from that point forward.

While I never did find overt references to her son in her diaries, other questions grew in my mind. Why did she write? Whom did she expect might read her words?

Soon I began to feel that I owed Hattie more, that she had a story or many stories to tell, and that, for whatever reason, I was the person chosen to tell them. I just didn't know how.

Fellow Wisconsin writer Christi Craig came to my rescue, suggesting the idea of writing flash narratives or vignettes based on Hattie's entries. These very short stories of a few hundred words allowed me to share snapshots of Hattie's life using her own voice, while trimming away the often unnecessary details of weather and daily work and aches and pains. I also culled lines of the diaries for found poetry, and shared both the narratives and poetry on my blog.

When I brought some of the pieces to my bi-weekly Red Oak Roundtable group for critique, I learned that I wasn't alone in writing about family letters and diaries. I asked Christi if she would be willing to see if there was enough interest for a book of such writing, as a co-editor. She said yes almost before I finished my question.

We asked for submissions of creative nonfiction, poetry, and essays inspired by family documents and objects such as diaries and letters, genealogical records, photographs, gravestones. Is there a single word for such a genre? The closest may be *ekphrasis* (EK-fruh-sis), a Greek term for literary description or commentary (usually poetry) of a work of art. One of the most famous and earliest examples of ekphrasis is the detailed description of the rings on the Shield of Achilles in Homer's *Iliad*: "Two cities radiant on the shield appear, / The image one of peace, and one of war...."

Ekphrasis can also occur in prose, such as in one of my favorite books, Willa Cather's *Song of the Lark*, in which the character of Thea visits the Art Institute of Chicago and finds a painting by Jules Adolphe Breton: "But in that same room there was a picture — oh, that was the thing she ran upstairs so fast to see! That was her picture. She imagined that nobody cared for it but herself, and that it waited for her." A more recent example from fiction is Donna Tartt's *The Goldfinch* and its use of the similarly titled painting (1654) by Carel Fabritius (Metropolitan Museum of Art): "...something about the neat, compact way it tucked down inside itself — its brightness, its alert watchful expression — made me think of pictures I'd seen of my mother when she was small: a dark-capped finch with steady eyes."

More broadly, ekphrasis can mean any work of art that describes or comments upon another work of art, and it is in this respect that I use the term here. In lieu of paintings and sculptures and more traditional art forms, our writers set their powers of observation on notebooks and diaries, photographs, letters, school certificates, genealogical records, tombstones, household silver, and other artifacts.

One danger of this very personal exploration of the past is sentimentality — an over-reliance on feeling at the expense of synthesis and insight. Related to sentimentality is an indulgence in what the late writer and scholar Svetlana Boym called *restorative nostalgia*, an overemphasis on tradition and homecoming, longing for a *restoration of what was* or a return to an idealized home or past that may have never existed.

In contrast, Boym described *reflective nostalgia*, which focuses on ambivalence and complexity. Reflective nostalgia allows for both feeling *and* critical thinking as we inhabit simultaneously then and now. Whereas restorative nostalgia is static, reflective nostalgia allows for personal growth and existential questioning. It is this second type of nostalgia that you will find in the pages that follow, as the authors open their minds and hearts to new ways of seeing themselves and the world, knowing that their explorations may bring them more questions than answers.

The works are organized alphabetically by author name. I would like to thank Christi for her keen eye and discriminating ear as she worked with the writers to edit their pieces. She has an uncanny knack for seeing fresh possibilities in a slightly changed phrase or rearranged paragraph, while honoring the original voice and intent. I could not have asked for a better partner in this venture.

About the Works

Kristine D. Adams starts us off with "Wally's World," inspired by her father-in-law's notebooks, and she challenges us to think of whose stories we may be called to tell: "If not you, who? And if not now, when?" In "When We Feel Invisible," **JoAnne Bennett** searches for shared DNA, "a father with no name," and "a connection to this invisible part of me." Letters from her immigrant ancestors allow **Aleta Chossek** to recreate her grandmother's arrival in Chicago in 1925 to begin "A New Life," while five years later and sixty miles from Chicago in Woodstock, Illinois, **Sally Cissna** also relies on letters to tell the story of her aunt and uncle and the scourge of tuberculosis in "Come Home, Peter." Continuing with the theme of illness and loss, **Gloria DiFulvio**'s "If She Had Lived" imagines an alternative life for her family, had her grandmother not died from the 1918 Spanish flu.

Julia Gimbel transforms pages of "a worn, black leather scrapbook" into "In a Sailor's Footsteps," the story of her father's experience of leaving home for the first time to fight in World War II. **Myles Hopper** returns to basement memories and a wrinkled grade school certificate in "Exodus Redux" as he reflects on exile, true love, and what has been gained and lost. To write "Tracing My Father's Admonition," **Margaret Krell** carries her father's stories to Dresden, seeking meaning in memory, words, and names. "Extract of Household Registration" is **Amy Wang Manning**'s search for solace in an English translation of a Taiwanese household registry, the only record she has of her father's family.

Nancy Martin, in "The Teetotaler," finds a new understanding of her father in his letters to his mother during World War II. From a treasure trove of papers and photos, **Patricia Ann McNair** pieces together her father's life as a motorcycle missionary in Korea at the start of the 20th century in "Climbing the Crooked Trails." **Carolou Nelsen** writes "I Had a Brother" as a collaboration with her big brother's war-time letters, while **Joanne Nelson**'s "In My Office" offers a dual perspective "of the little girl held close by her brothers in a corner of the kitchen...and of the woman at her desk in a basement office."

A great-aunt's genealogical record allows **Annilee Newton** to bring to life her grandfather "Leet," and she realizes "I don't know what to call the in-between parts that aren't there anymore." **Pam Parker** opens "The Blue Cardboard Box" to find letters and answers to painful questions about a grandmother she never met. **Ramona M. Payne** gets to know a mother-in-law whom she saw only twice and never talked to in "Without Words." In "She Wrote a Good Letter," **Valerie Reynolds** recalls meeting her husband through letters before they ever spoke a word to each other.

Jessica Schnur strings together personal and family memories of her mother to deliver a "Schnur Family Announcement." **Meagan Schultz**'s "They Were Young Once, Too" tells the love story of her grandparents through the gift of their letters to each other. **Yvonne Stephens** uses letters to create the found poems "Syl" and "Letters on Repeat from 728 W Spruce St." The microfiction piece "Wind the Fabric Tighter" by **Kim Suhr** weaves the story of an unknown "girl in a casket with a halo of flowers, her posthumous portrait the only proof she'd lived."

In the final piece, **Julie Anne Thorndyke** discovers in "Aunt Becker's Secret" a kindred spirit in "the memory of those eyes and their piercing gaze, daring me to be myself, daring me to surmount all obstacles and be the writer she recognized in the bookish child she saw before her." May we all have such a kindred spirit and be one ourselves.

Family Stories from the Attic

Kristine D. Adams lives near enough to the Ohio River to hear barge traffic. An author, speaker, and writing coach, she founded "What's Your Story?" Writing Workshop series in order to help people elevate their sense of purpose and recognize their impact with others. Adams studied journalism and design before changing her academic focus to psychology and behavior analysis. Her published writing appeared in commercial and nonprofit media, regional newspapers, and online journals. She's a featured presenter across several states. Visit her website at www.kdadams.com.

When our children were still in school, my husband and I attempted something like a Findhorn community/"back to the land" experience. We bought land in the Missouri Ozarks where we grew preposterously big gardens, planted trees, and engaged with nearby neighbors. We raised rabbits, chickens, ducks, and geese, and adopted a Morgan-cross colt.

Stories my husband's family shared about their farm experiences thirty-some years earlier eclipsed our tie-dyed attempts to live close to the land. The U.S. economy seemed at cross-purposes with the nation's farmers, despite their vital role producing food for our country. When our kids entered college, we found city jobs. As a social work liaison for struggling families, my awareness widened — my writing reflected the changes.

Eventually, extended family members learned I was writing. "You'll need to be our historian, you realize," some said — I resisted. Packets gradually began to arrive in my roadside mailbox, some from people I scarcely knew, shared with hopes I would be a good caretaker for them.

The notebooks from Wallace Grant Adams have changed me. His words, as lean as the man himself, serve to open times I'll never see. Thankfully, he also took thousands of slides, kept safe and dry in the Arizona climate. It's my honor and privilege to introduce this lovely man, with thanks to Christi Craig, Lisa Rivero, and Hidden Timber Books.

BY KRISTINE D. ADAMS

Wally's World

G iven a choice, Wally probably would prefer to remain off-stage. In a quite real sense, he has indeed made his final exit. But since his rich journals have come to my hands, I'm obligated to share them, and to share *him*.

If only I could add the deep timbre of his voice, the funny intake of breath when he chuckled with amusement. Those remain embedded in my mind and heart, even while the sound of my mother's singing and laughter is lost to me.

From the moment I opened Wally's steno notebook, in single sheet records I witnessed an America built with grit, self-reliance, and the will to work alongside nature and its inhabitants. Understated nobility shines through his rigorous work ethic, an obvious necessity common among his neighbors. His personal drive and range of keen interest in people and places appear on every page — he remained always a student of life.

Wallace Grant Adams left his Iowa family farm in 1929 for good — his own good — defying stern admonishment from his daddy. Wearied by the weight of being indispensable, sunup until well past sundown, his spirit chafed inside of him.

Yet his writing never tends toward bitterness.

He channeled his energies into complex projects with a practical, summary lens on his days. At moments of rest, his mind stayed busy, as reflected in the pages of his journals.

...Got new Sears catalogue today... Worked crosswords... Took old motorcycle magnets apart. Demonstrated magnetic field to Uncle Horatio...

Soon after, this: "Plowed all day. Saw a swallow." I picture his upright stride slowing a bit, as he covers ground losing color in the fading light. Before he enters the farmhouse, his spirit finds a flash of relief in the bird's wheeling arc.

Yearning for something beyond Iowa farmlands, he dreamed of becoming a pilot. Although it doesn't appear on his pages, in conversation around the table Wally later recalled a particular exchange. He and his brother Martin, walking in from fields with their father, Theron, noticed a flock of birds soar across a sky lit by sunset. Wally lifted his eyes and sighed. "Ah, I'd love to be able to fly like that."

His father retorted, "Ha! If God intended man to fly, He'd have given him wings!" The subject would stay closed. By and by, in time carved from his daily routine, Wally drove to a small airfield and took pilot lessons in secret. Eventually, he'd fly his own Ronca Cub plane to Iowa, from the adopted home he chose years later in Arizona.

But Wyoming marked the start of the hiatus that separated him from life as family farmhand. To get himself West, he rode the rails as a hobo, across flat Iowa fields, mountains, and gritty desert basins. Wally drank deeply of his new life. The untouched, ever-changing landscape captivated his keen artistic eye, whetting lifelong intimacy with the earth.

He made it to Laramie Plains, where he cowboyed with his Grant cousins for several years. The Grants' "Snowshoe Ranch" originally encompassed 150,000 acres. First ceded in the late 1800s to Ulysses Simpson Grant—yes, a descended cousin of *that* Ulysses S. Grant—and Frances Sofia Adams, the land required proof of regular improvement for ownership. The deed's ninety-nine year lease required payments of one dollar per year!

Wally delighted in the camaraderie of hard-working men and even the spare bunkhouse quarters. He regularly rode and maintained the out-fence of the ranch, reduced by the early 1930s to a mere 127,000 acres. In time, he also worked as trail postman, picking up canvas mailbags in Casper, Wyoming, each month. Riding horseback, he made deliveries to ranches across a hundred-mile circuit. A few years into his adventure, he returned east, wooed and wed the girl he'd left behind in Nevada, Iowa.

Wally's transition from independent cowboy to husband and father must have been a struggle, particularly given the political and economic constraints of time and place. The Great Depression was just ending by 1935, when he and his bride, Vilda, began married life in a tiny converted machine shed on the family farm. After early attention to livestock and equipment maintenance, Wally "...thawed water, plastered walls" insulated with fresh hay and lath strips. Two days later he "wallpapered all day. Slow." Soon after, "...Went to Ames for Sears delivery, new linoleum. Rex came, bro't cookstove and set it up. One load of wood in." Their happy home, just one room — though its shelves and rug wouldn't come until completion of spring planting.

The newlyweds enjoyed the company of younger brother Martin, a bachelor who remained in the family home all of his life. His playful, light-hearted nature helped ease Wally's abrupt return to farming. Journal entries shed shafts of light on their evenings and recreation:

Drove to Ames, took skates to be sharpened. Played checkers until late.

Up early to Cambridge, ran John Deere show. Jordans' for party at the Grange, home 2:30 a.m. Morning blizzard, stayed in.

Doubtless in my mind, the respite created by Mother Nature likely allowed for a second pot of coffee, and little more. I imagine he spent time working out problem-solving diagrams during those side-blown snowstorms, sketched on old newspapers. The knees of Wally's heavy denims always wore thin — never the side with back pockets!

Martin discovered, after a particularly rugged winter, that squirrels had buried hundreds of walnuts throughout the ground near the farm-house. Rather than sacrifice emerging seedlings to the mower blade, he dug them up, repotted and set them aside. Once the trees gained size enough to be viable, Martin trucked the lot to the local Boy Scouts troop, to help with Arbor Day celebrations. He would later bequeath a sizable trust to establish tree management in the area — a legacy that continues today. But the brothers also created homespun fun:

Built scrap wood Chinese Checkers game. Martin layed out grid, I drilled out divots by hand. Got our old marble bag to try it out.

Martin's sunny perspective must have lightened any job the brothers tackled. And they tackled plenty.

Wally's description of a single day, recorded in matter-of-fact tone, includes "...took stock across river." Research determined what his simple statement meant. He and his brother, with their aging father, walked and "yahooed" a number of cows (exact count not cited) from their cozy barn, across windy fields, then into half-frozen water — and out the other side — on January 2, 1939. On foot.

That same day, Wally "...finished wiring house, soldered splices and taped them...made oil barrel stove with Martin..." and then completed routine farm chores.

He found weekend work in the village of Nevada, Iowa, at the only theatre within miles, as projectionist. His thorough record of film titles and cast suggests an insight to one nourishing diversion — brief respite in the opportunity to revel in popular cowboy tales and glamorous Hollywood movie spectacles of the time.

But Wally's interest in budding technologies didn't end there. His work as a projectionist soon led to launching a circuit theatre. Driving a 1930s touring car, he brought heavy film reels produced in distant California to the hayseed flatlands. In early evenings, he left the warmth and comfort of home, driving to neighboring farms. The much-welcomed films then were projected onto sheets inside barns. The price of admission: a nickel.

Through Wally's journal pages, a catalogue of early film history appears — along with its challenges. He lists the shows:

Made signs for 'Cowboy and the Lady,' Gary Cooper & Merle Oberon' – 'Hold That Co-ed,' John Barrymore, Joan Davis, – 'Racket Busters,' Humphrey Bogart – 'Cowboy from Brooklyn,' Dick Powell & Priscilla Lane with 2 shorts, 'Vitaphone Follies' & 'Katnip Kollege.'

After the entry of 'Romance of the Limberlost,' Jean Parker & Marjorie Main, he writes of trouble.

Burned out projection bulb & projection leader on reel three went up in smoke. (So much smoke.)

The flammable cellulose could easily have ended in theatre disaster, but for his quick thinking. Just a few pages later, this contrast:

Fed hogs, ground corn and hay, plowed, plastered main room. Show: 'Just Around the Corner,' Shirley Temple.

Wally's very own dimpled blonde came into his life during this time, a baby daughter. His writing became clipped, suggesting fewer stolen moments. Those journal passages continue to paint a happy man, living his life consumed with clean and meaningful work, pockets of fun and a newborn's laughter.

He discovered an innate ability with photography and taught himself to make prints from individual film cells. Months later, acquiring a camera, Wally became a portrait photographer with his bride's assistance, hand-tinting the prints using dyes and brushes. And somehow, through his changing times of dutiful son to independent man, from husband and farmer to photographer and so much more, he was always a writer.

His notebooks, in careful, economic penmanship, describe with Bob Cratchett-like detail the events of overfull days. Every page, front and back, is filled, written in a steady hand that would have made his one-room schoolteacher proud. The staggering scope of skills Wally and his brother Martin used to maintain the large farm holdings, coupled with a grinding moral weight of daily, obligatory tasks, seems impossible. Their hands-on approach mastered every challenge, not only of necessity but drawing on fundamental self-reliance. Where and when he found opportunity to write the journals, no one has been able to guess!

As a teacher of writing, I partner with Wally and encourage people to write personal stories. I project a page from his journal and read aloud through just two or three days' activities. Although his intent was clearly to record progress on specific tasks, his everyman tone reaches out, more powerfully than a documentary of the time. The language — like Wally — is never showy, nor do his words convey a hint of complaint. The record of his work is stunning.

And I ask participants, "Who will tell what *you* know about someone like Wally?"

Invariably the room quiets, and I gather that the writers might be thinking of loved ones. A faraway focus comes to their eyes, a softening in many faces. Perhaps they recall a handmade quilt, a family cradle, or the way an uncle whistled when he worked. The legacies linger in watercolor memories of worn tools, cozy rooms, songs sung in slow harmony.

And finally, repeating an early adjuration from my program to harvest memories, another slide appears. It reads:

"If not you, who? And if not now, when?"

From the beautiful Pacific Northwest, JoANNE BENNETT has raised her three wonderful daughters, now married, alongside her supportive husband of forty-one years. Although her life journey has been difficult at times, she loves focusing on her passion — writing. Her heartfelt desire as an author is to reach out and encourage others never to give up on discovering their gifts. JoAnne's work has appeared in a number of print and online publications over the years. Her most recent contribution is in an anthology, *I Am Free* (2016), and her favorite piece is about making a difference in the lives of young people in the book, *Dear Wonderful You* (2014).

I don't know why I put so much faith in small-town gossip, but for over twenty years, that is just what I did. I thought that submitting my DNA to commercial test companies would give me further supporting evidence of my birth family, based until that point upon mostly hearsay and a random Christmas card with an obituary tucked inside. I didn't think it mattered that, on my paternal side, I was connecting only to DNA matches many generations removed.

Then I received notification from someone who wanted to share information. Nothing could have prepared me for what would forever change my life. He ended up being my half-brother — listed number one on my list of DNA matches. This is why so many of my matches weren't connecting with anyone: they were related to his father's side of the family. A DNA expert explained that a red flag should have been that I couldn't get the other presumed birth father to connect to any of my matches closer than with seventh great-grandparents. "Going that far back, the DNA gets diluted and isn't a true indicator of anything," she explained. DNA doesn't lie. The two of us indeed share the same biological father, and many of my DNA matches now connect to my real birth father on my family tree.

I certainly would have never imagined that there had always been a different, miraculous (and welcomed) ending to my story.

BY JoAnne Bennett

When We Feel Invisible
A Flash Memoir

WHEN I THOUGHT OF MY BIOLOGICAL FATHER, the same image played over and over. A silhouette far in the distance, a man walking away from me into a cloud of dust kicked up by the small, Nevada mining town. Here, the slow-motion picture always blurred. I needed to know if he ever looked back.

I remember when I learned I had been born from infidelity. My father had no name and I felt ashamed, less valuable, unseen. I sought the connection to this invisible part of me, searched for belonging in some full, sheltering family tree where my name could hang, took a DNA test. Once a small rock skipping gently over the water, I am now part of a bigger ripple: ancestors continue to show up. Shared DNA.

No longer am I a mistake. No longer an empty chair at family gatherings. The stigma of small-town gossip erased by old photos and kind gestures, life stories. I finally found what I lost. My history. No longer invisible.

ALETA CHOSSEK is finding new life through writing. Daring to share family stories with others primarily through Red Oak Roundtables and Judy Bridges' Writing Workshops has opened for Aleta a world of connected human experience and joy. Writing allows Aleta to reflect on lessons from her family, travel, and working with the people of a small area in Tanzania. A wife, sister, mother, and grandmother, she tries to follow the advice of the poet Mary Oliver: "Pay attention, Be astonished, Tell about it." Read Aleta's blog at aletameru.wordpress.com.

"A New Life, New York to Chicago" is part of the account of my maternal grandmother, Kristine Kristiansen, and my mother, Odny, traveling from a small town on the West coast of Norway to Kristine's husband — my grandfather, Fredrik Hjelmeland. Married in Norway, my grandfather had preceded my grandmother to the United States to prepare for her to join him in building a life together. Their reunion was delayed by the birth of my mother.

"A New Life" tells of my grandmother's anticipation of that reunion and lifts up a fragment of the immigrant experience. I am so fortunate to have multiple written primary sources. My grandfather's letters home to his sisters and brothers have been preserved and translated from Norwegian. A smaller number from my grandmother survive. One letter provides the opening quote of this piece. In addition, I am able to quote from essays my mother, Odny Hjelmeland Reckling, wrote when she was a student at St. Olaf College from 1942 to 1946. The essays quoted in "A New Life" are part of interviews she recorded with her parents. Finally, I have the benefit of oral history and photos. I traveled several times to my grandparents and mother's home in Norway, the first time with my maternal grandmother, Kristine. It is my goal through this writing to share with future generations of my family the strength of spirit that is their heritage and the fascinating people who came before them.

BY ALETA CHOSSEK

A New Life

New York to Chicago

"And now I have started a new life, quite different from what I had before. All of a sudden I have a large family! April 1, Kristine, Odny and Alf came to Chicago. We stayed there for a night at a hotel, and we came to Waukegan, April 2. I guess they were pretty happy when they saw us and the long journey was finally over. Do you remember Mikal, the first day we arrived in Chicago?"

~ Fredrik Hjelmeland, Waukegan, Illinois, in a letter to his brother, F. Mikal Hjelmeland, in Norway. April 15, 1925

O n the morning of the eighth day, they woke to quiet. The ship was not rocking. Faintly, Kristine could hear some shouting and banging but no engines clanking or roaring. They had docked.

America, New York, now she would see what she had only heard about. Relief mingled with excitement and fear. Everything that could be done was done. Kristine had laid out their traveling clothes the night before. She peeked out of the stateroom to see that the big suitcase she set out last night was already gone. As she bustled around getting herself ready before Odny, eleven months old, woke up, she worried about how she would manage getting from the boat to the train with only Fredrik's nineteen-year-old nephew, Alf, to help her. They would carry a travel basket and small valise. Fearing she would miss their train and be alone in the big city of New York, she was nearly pacing the tiny room.

When she finished washing herself and brushing her hair, she woke Odny to feed her before dressing them both. Odny wore a plain smock, fresh knit stockings, sturdy shoes, and a coat and hat. Kristine's own traveling outfit was similar, brown and practical. She knew that they would be in these clothes at least two days. Since she didn't know if it would be mild and spring-like or still wintry, she hoped their Norwegian wools would be warm enough. After processing through immigration, they were to get a bus to Grand Central Station for the twenty-hour train trip to Chicago.

At breakfast, she sipped her coffee and pushed around a piece of bread and cheese, too excited to eat anything more. Her shipboard friend, Inge, tried to reassure her.

"Kristine, once you are settled, you must bring your husband back to New York, to Brooklyn. I'll bet he knows some of the Norwegians in our neighborhood," she said.

"I wish you could go with us, Inge. You've been such a help to me. Is Chicago far from here?"

"Oh, it's far but the NAL, Norwegian American Line, has you booked all the way through. I'll make sure that you and your nephew get in the immigration line before I say good-bye. Then once you are processed, just look for the NAL bus to Grand Central Station." After they got in the line and Inge gave her farewell, Kristine clutched her daughter in her arms and her paperwork in her bag.

Before we could leave the boat in New York, we were to have a physical examination. However, my mother and I only had our eyes examined. ~ Odny Hjelmeland, St. Olaf College essay, 1943

The first step was to fall into two lines — men in one and women and children in another — for a physical by American officials, all men. When it was their turn, Kristine stepped up to a rough looking man with a white coat. He took hold of her chin, jerked her head side to side, looked in her eyes and then into Odny's. After he wrote on her papers, he thrust them at her and said something she didn't understand. "You're OK, lucky to be here. Next!" Not until the woman behind her pushed her away, did she understand that not only were her papers OK but that they had passed the "physical exam." People talked so loud and so fast, she couldn't understand a word.

Passport for Kristine Hjelmeland & Odny

Alf had been taken out of the men's line and had gone behind a screen to be examined more thoroughly. As she moved to the departure deck, she worried that he would be detained. How would she ever find her way without him to help? She looked for another passenger who might help her locate Alf but saw no one she knew. She chose a place to wait near the rail where she thought he would see her. Despite her layers of wool clothing, she shivered in the raw wind from the harbor. As she tried to distract Odny from squirming by looking to the pier at carriages, horse drawn and motor, and the stevedores unloading the ship, Alf found them.

"Thank goodness you have come," Kristine said, relieved to have Alf's solid presence next to her. He took Odny from her arms and spun her around.

"Look at all the people little one. We are in America!" Alf was jubilant, not overwhelmed at all by the people and bustle on the dock. His excitement renewed Kristine.

Soon, they, too, made their way in the steadily moving line down the gangplank and onto American soil. The clamor and surge of so many people kept them moving through the processing hall and on to find their baggage, but as much as she had dreamt about this moment, she couldn't really take it all in. Once they were on the NAL bus that took them from the docks to the train station, the driver told Alf where to look for the train to Chicago. Kristine hoped that Alf understood enough English to lead them through even more crowds with their trunks and baggage to the right place.

From the open windows of the motor bus she took in the muddy streets and breathed in the stench of open sewers running alongside the roadway. Ragged children held the hands of tired looking women while passing shops outside of the Bowery on their way up to the train station. Kristine pulled Odny even closer on her lap. Alf told her the many-storied dingy buildings on either side were apartments for the poor called "tenements."

By contrast, Grand Central Station seemed luxurious and enormous. From the gilded entrance at the carriage drive where the bus dropped them off to the echoing Great Hall, Kristine looked for the tracks that would take them away. Important looking men in dark suits and overcoats hurried as they crisscrossed from one side of the arching hallway to the other. While uniformed workers behind wrought iron ticket windows called out departing trains, porters vied to help with their trunks.

"We do not have much time until the train, *tante*. I will get the trunk and suitcases checked in and you must take Odny to the platform of the New York Central to Chicago." Alf shouted over the din. "*Tante*, can you do that?"

"I think so but how will you know which car we are in? What if you don't get on the right one?"

"I will be able to run if I have to but you cannot with the baby. Just get on the train. Find our compartment and I'll find you."

While we were on the train, carrying us to Chicago, we were supposed to have a sleeper. It was all paid for, but we never got it, and we couldn't do any complaining because Mother couldn't talk Eng-

lish and neither could I. My mother tells me that she literally carried me from Norway to Chicago. ~ Odny, St. Olaf College essay

Getting to the right track for the train to Chicago didn't seem so simple. Kristine checked the numbers on the tickets and studied the signs. Not knowing English, she ignored the remarks from passersby swirling around her as she stood still in the midst of so much activity. At the New York Central Platform #12, she found a stocky man in a navy blue uniform directing people. She showed him her tickets. Odny wiggled in her arms. When the man waved her toward seats in a car, she tried to ask about a *seng*, a bed. No one understood her, so she found two seats together and let Odny stand until the train began to move. Alf found her only after the train had left the big station.

"Alf, you're here! It did not go well without your English. I tried to make them understand we are to have a bed. I showed two different men my ticket but I think they told me to sit here," she said. "What should I have done?"

"I don't know. My little English is not enough for all these questions. Maybe when they collect the tickets later, we can move. At least I think we are on the right train," Alf said and sat down next to her.

Side by side on little more than a bench with a wooden back, they sat, looking out the window at tall buildings, railroads and shipyards, factories and warehouses. They crossed bridges and slowed for some crossings. Dirty puddles and patches of ice littered the muddy roads that crossed the tracks. Lost in a muddle of dark thoughts, neither Kristine nor Alf had anything to talk about.

After a half hour, a conductor came by and punched their tickets. They tried to ask about a sleeper compartment but the only English word they could come up with was bed. The conductor hardly slowed down, shaking his head as he moved to the next passenger.

Alf looked at Kristine and saw her eyes squeezed shut. "Are you all right?" he asked.

"I'm very tired, will you take a walk with Odny? Just the length of the car?" Her voice quavered but she did not allow the tears to fall.

"Sure, I can use a stretch, you rest for a few minutes." Alf carried the little girl up and down the aisle of the railroad car until she fell asleep against his shoulder. He sat down and gently shifted her to Kristine's arms. They settled in, gazing out the window, not talking, trying to rest like the napping Odny.

Once they left the buildings behind, the land was flat and not green. No fjords or mountains broke up the late March landscape. The steam and soot from the locomotive gave a gray cast to the windows that they peered through. The cloudy afternoon turned to an early dusk. Kristine had not expected it to be so dismal. Throughout the night, Kristine's head fell forward onto her chest and jerked back as the train steamed its way through town after town. Odny whimpered, even as she slept in her arms. How she wished she had known enough English to get the sleeper car that Fredrik had said was included in her passage.

A man in front of them had smoked a cigar since he got on at a stop during the night in a place called Pittsburgh. Kristine stirred from her fitful sleep when the woman across from her pulled a jar of something that smelled of onions and cabbage from a yellow tapestry bag. She watched in dismay as the woman dug into the jar with her fingers for her breakfast. Kristine rubbed her forehead and breathed into her fine white handkerchief. Her head ached from the sour smell, the smoke, and too many bodies on the noisy train. For reprieve, she, Odny, and Alf went to the dining car where their tickets got them a breakfast of dry white bread and coffee. There was no milk or farina for a baby. How good it was that Odny was still nursing.

After twenty hours of sitting in this stiff, upright seat, she was tired, dusty, and a little nauseated. Odny needed a bath. In the wash-room, she had tried to rinse out diapers but there was not much she could do with so little water, not even heated. Their bundle of soiled diapers and clothes was growing in the bottom of Kristine's travel valise. What would Fredrik think when they got to Chicago? She had so wanted his first meeting with his daughter to be perfect. She'd never imagined America was so dirty, gray, gritty. She'd begun to feel as if she'd made a terrible mistake.

After the ship, where everyone had some connection with Norway, she longed for someone other than Alf to talk to, but all the people on the train spoke English or another language. Alf had gone quiet, too. She wondered if he was just tired or nervous.

The man in the blue uniform came through shouting something she didn't understand until he said, "Chicago." Dozing in his seat next to hers, Alf shook himself awake. In his broken English, he asked the gruff man across the aisle what the conductor had announced. An hour to Chicago! This town with the ugly smoke stacks and sulfur smells was someplace called Gary.

Kristine was wide-awake now. She handed the baby to Alf, who held her in front of him, like a bag of oats, gripping her little shoulders. Digging in their belongings, Kristine found a clean dress and hand-knitted stockings for Odny and a fresh collar for the blouse she had put on before leaving the ship yesterday morning. She took Odny from Alf and stood in line for the washroom.

The brakes screamed as the train slowed. It seemed as if they were underground — no sky, no trees, no town visible. Where were they? They had been told they were coming into Union Station, brand new and the biggest station in the United States. To Kristine, it looked like a giant, steel cave.

A new building for trains was not on Kristine's mind for long as she leaned forward in her seat, peering out the grimy windows. Suddenly, she saw Fredrik before the train fully stopped; she sighed a breath she did not know she had been holding. He really was here. He would take care of them in this strange place. Who was that fellow standing next to him?

My father and Ben Hjelmeland, a boyhood chum of my father, who also lived on the Hjelmeland farm, met us at the station in Chicago on April 1, 1925. ~ Odny, St. Olaf College essay

"Union Station, Chicago, Illinois," the conductor bellowed. Alf stood up and pushed his way to make a path among all the other passengers. He carried the two suitcases while Kristine followed with Odny and her travel basket.

As she took the porter's hand to step over the tracks onto the train platform, she felt Fredrik reach for Odny. She tumbled into him, handing him their daughter.

"You're really here!" Kristine cried.

"Finally, you have come," Fredrik answered.

"This is Odny. Odny, this is your daddy."

"She's beautiful, you're beautiful."

"Can you smile for your daddy?"

Nearly two years since they had married, over a year since they had been together, they clung to one another as a family, laughing and crying at the same time, an island among the bustling hub-bub of travelers being met, taxis being arranged and luggage handled.

Fredrik introduced his friend Ben, who happened to be working in Chicago. Alf shook Ben's hand while asking question after question about work, women, and life in Chicago, thrilled to meet another Norwegian man, young and single. The younger men took charge of getting the trunks while Fredrik led his little family to a shiny sedan. Kristine was awe-struck.

"Fredrik, whose car is this?" she asked.

"It is mine, Kristine. It was new when I came to Waukegan two years ago. Do you like it?"

"Yes, of course, but you own it? You can go wherever you want?" she asked.

"Well, there are not so many good roads. I can't take it on some of these farm paths but most places, yes, I can go where I want when I want," Fredrik said with a proud smile. Kristine had never ridden in a privately owned automobile, only taxis in Bergen. No one in Forde had a car yet. It was hard for her to believe this was her husband's car that she could ride in every day.

From Union Station, Fredrik first drove them to a hotel where they could clean up and have some private time. The sixty miles to Waukegan on unpaved roads was too far to go before dark. Having finally gotten his wife and baby daughter to Chicago, he wouldn't risk spending their first night stuck in a rut on the muddy road to Waukegan.

As tired as she was, the energy of Chicago thrilled Kristine. While Odny napped, she bathed from the skin out and changed into clean clothes. When she emerged from the bathroom, Fredrik took her in his arms.

"Kristine, I have dreamt of this day, but holding you is so much better than my dreams. Thank you for coming. I prayed you would."

"You are my husband, Odny is our daughter. We should be together, we are a family," she whispered, shy of this man whom she had spent so little time with.

They took us to a café and mother thought the cups were much too
big and clumsy. She was used to the fine China ware in Norway.
~ Odny, St. Olaf College essay

Odny woke and it was time to go to a neighborhood café for supper. As they walked a few blocks to the café, Kristine and Alf peppered Fredrik with questions.

"Are the gas street lights on all night?"

"Where are all these people going?"

"How many streetcars are there? Where do they all go?"

"How many stories are these building? What kind of work is done there?"

So much to look at, to ask about. Fredrik carried Odny along while he answered their questions. She clung to his neck, fascinated by the lights and noise. Kristine teared up, so relieved that her baby and handsome husband liked each other. Doubts about leaving her friends in Norway, being in America, learning a new language faded as she felt Fredrik's hand on her back, guiding her, cherishing his baby, speaking lovingly in Norwegian. They walked for two blocks along a brick sidewalk with cars and streetcars passing by. Fredrik stopped where storefront windows shone with the glow from hanging electric bulbs.

"This is the café where we will have some *kveldsmat*, evening food," he announced.

As they opened the glass doors, Kristine took in the long narrow room, the assortment of painted tables, and bare wooden floor. Rugged looking men sat one or two to a table, bent over plates of food. "Fredrik," she whispered. "I don't know if we should be here. There are no women."

He looked around, seeming surprised that she was right. He had eaten here before and had bid on installing the electric lights. It was a working man's place if you weren't living at a boarding house. Fredrik had expected to see these ruddy faced fellows in dungarees with rolled up shirt sleeves bent over their plates, shoveling in food without much chatter. He hadn't realized that Kristine had never really seen laborers indoors, in a café.

As their little group stood trying to decide what to do, a round, cushiony woman with a full white apron over her flowered dress bustled out of a back room.

"Hello, welcome. Are you here for supper? We have ham tonight on our blue plate special," she said.

"Ja, that sounds good," Fredrik told her and introduced Kristine, Alf, and Odny.

The proprietress seated them at one of the painted wooden tables, all the while chattering away about how nice it was to have a family come from time to time. One bold fellow asked Fredrik how he had gotten so lucky. Others broke out laughing. Kristine shrank from the attention. The bright light, the bare tables, and snickers from the men made her feel conspicuous, not knowing what was funny. Kristine examined the heavy knife, fork, and soup spoon laid out on the table. Their hostess returned with three mugs of coffee and a piece of soft bread for Odny to chew on.

"Shall I bring the baby some mashed potatoes?" she asked.

Kristine didn't understand the question and Fredrik didn't know what babies ate, so they all looked politely at one another until he nodded. By the time he'd translated for Kristine, the woman had returned to the kitchen.

When the food came, they all got the same thing: a good sized piece of dry looking ham with a roll perched on it, mashed potatoes, and waxed beans all served on one plate with a blue stripe around the edge. Sipping her coffee from the mug made of the same heavy ceramic as the plate, Kristine thought of supper in her childhood home where she and her mother would have served smoked fish, flatbrod, cheese and fruit, where kaffe did not come with the meal and men did not sit in their shirt sleeves. Suddenly, she felt very far away from Norway. Her new life — creating a family, being a wife, making a home — was beginning.

"A new life, quite different from what [they] had before."

Fredrik and Kristine Hjelmeland and daughters
Odny (standing) and Ruth (circa 1940)

SALLY CISSNA is a retired communications professor, minister, engineer, and perpetual student. She comes from a family of letter writers and packrats, who have left a treasure trove of letters and other documents which she has collected over the years. Besides being the family archivist, she enjoys working on family trees, communicating with friends and family on Facebook, remodeling the home she shares with her spouse of 25 years and a zoo of fuzzy four-leggeds, and refurbishing her Yellow Route 66 PT Cruiser. She also volunteers as a photographer and Facebook coordinator for Repairers of the Breach Homeless Resource Center in her hometown of Milwaukee, Wisconsin. Read her blog, "Just Sayin'," at sallycissna.wordpress.com.

The letters in this essay are all genuine and addressed to my aunt and uncle, Helen and Henry Stolldorf. For forty-five years, Henry was a Lutheran minister in Lafayette, where they lived the entirety of their adult lives. Both were born in Woodstock, Illinois, and the letters are from Helen's family in Woodstock, mainly her mother, Ida, and her sisters, Mame (Marion — my mother) and Edna (Ed). I was born twenty years later, so this is the story of Mame's first family, husband Peter, children Maryon and Bobbi, and one very important year of their lives at the very beginning of the Great Depression, when the economic strains on the middle-class, small-town family are just beginning to be felt. In a time when penicillin was not readily available, when men were discouraged from spitting on the sidewalk for fear of spreading tuberculosis, and when many of the life-saving vaccines were yet to be discovered, the weekly letters always include news on the health of family members. In 1930, most of the worry was about Peter, Mame's husband, who was a resident at the La Salle Tuberculosis Sanatorium in Ottawa, Illinois.

BY SALLY CISSNA

Come Home, Peter

"You got what?" Ida Wienke said sharply.

"Got laid off," her husband, John, answered sheepishly.

"Well, what does that mean?" Ida did not abide reticence. "Is it temporary? Will you be called back?"

John shuffled slightly, and then, looking down, said, "Fired. That's what it means."

John remembered that three years earlier he had been the one who pushed Ida, insisting that they sell their bakery, with its 3:00 A.M. wake-up call and exhausting work schedule, for a steadier income at the expanding Woodstock Typewriter Company. He had argued that they weren't getting any younger. This year he would be sixty and Ida fifty-five. Since the children were all but grown, their rooms could soon be filled with boarders, and Ida would have her hands full without middle-of-the-night baking. But now, only three years later — 1930 — everything had changed.

"Great! What a wonderful New Year's gift! What shall we do now?" She drew out the word "shall" ironically, grabbed the skillet from the lower cupboard, and banged it down on the stove. Supper would be simple. A stew filled with leftovers from the week. A bit of shredded beef, potatoes, onions, some carrots, string beans and a pickled cucumber and onion salad canned last summer, and, of course, bread, coffee, and milk.

"I have to get supper. The children will be home soon." She turned her back, signaling the conversation was over, and began cutting up vegetables. "Go entertain the babies."

The monotony of cooking allowed thinking. What would they do? Three incomes would still be coming into the household at 365 Lincoln Avenue. Ed had a steady job at the Woodstock Public Library as Assistant Librarian, which was good for a twenty-three-year-old and should be secure, one would think, even in a downturn. People would surely want to read more as they work less. She smirked. Ed... Dorothea Edna, a somewhat difficult, even petulant, child grown into a hard-working, albeit somewhat peevish, adult, hated her name and so picked Ed...Ed!...a boy's name! Ida shook her head.

Bob...soon out of high school and only months until he goes to Purdue with a scholarship! His part-time job with the Woodstock Gardens will help a little. Ida smiled, her anger dissipating. He was going to make them proud, just as Helen and Henry had.

First-born, clear-thinking, and smart, Helen had wanted to write a homemaker's column for a newspaper, but then she met dear, hand-some Henry. When Henry was called as pastor of Trinity Lutheran Church, what was Helen to do but marry him and go with him to Lafayette, Indiana. At twenty-six years old, they had been young for such an assignment, but both were energetic and committed. Ida would have given anything for just a little of that energy. Helen was now a pastor's wife, so her degree in home economics was being put to good use, even if she never got to write her column. Helen and Henry made such a comely couple, suited to one another in many ways, but married three years and no children yet, a bit strange. Ida frowned. Another thing to worry about.

And Marion...their Mame...their sickly child. First her tonsils poisoned her and then rheumatic fever almost killed her, resulting in St. Vitus Dance, the jerking and lurching when she walked. Couldn't hold on to a pen at times, but she had finished high school, the tremors easing in her senior year. And in her twenty-second year, sandy-haired Peter Rasmussen plucked her right off her stool at the bakery, with his sly way of showing up on the afternoons she worked, asking for pumpernickel bread while knowing full well it was gone by 10:00 A.M. As Ida chopped carrots, fresh from the sand crock in the basement, she smiled at the image of the two of them...Mame, with her gray-hazel eyes, brown hair cut in a short stylish bob, perched on a stool, sketch book in her lap, and tousled-hair Peter in clean bib overalls, tall and handsome with those dancing Danish-blue eyes, leaning on the counter, teasing her. Their wedding was simply beautiful, out under the trees at Pete's farm. The fresh air of the country and the farm work improved Mame's health and made her stronger. Good thing they started their life together at a run, Ida mused. Two children in two years, little Maryon, now two and a quarter, and Bobby, thirteen months. But all that was before Pete's weakness and pain overwhelmed him. Tuberculosis. Ida stopped peeling and stared out the window.

"We have no choice," she had said to Peter's parents, Jenny and Sam. "We have to get the children out of that house." Peter quickly moved to his parents' house, and, later, to the Sanitarium in Ottawa. And Mame and the two babies came home, taking the two front rooms upstairs. Big enough for them, until Peter got better. The animals, equipment, and farm were sold, and Mame got a job at Wiem's Department Store down on the square. It doesn't pay a lot, but she was twenty-five with no experience except milking cows and selling at the bakery, and beggars can't be choosers. And Ida became a full-time grandma. She sighed again, resuming her work, summing up her reverie, resolving that they would just have to pool money until Papa could find something.

Friday Evening – April 18, 1930
Woodstock, Illinois

Dear Helen and Henry,

What has become of you both? Ed & I have wondered all this week if you were both sick and unable to write. Hope you have only been busy or negligent.

The children are fine and play so nice all day long only when they are tired or hungry do they fuss.

Bob is out of a job. The grafting and potting came to an end and now they are beginning on entirely new work but laid off quite a number. Bob was to have work but evidently someone told the main boss that he was going to school in the fall and when the boss asked him, he, like a nice truthful boy, said that he was and as there is a lot to learn in the coming work, I suppose they weren't going to train someone who didn't intend to stay.

Uncle Herman is going to give him some work soon. It isn't much money and maybe won't last long but at least it will be something.

I'm trying to sew a little but accomplish so little. I guess I'm getting old.

Bye-bye for now and do let me know all is well!

Love from us all, Mother

The kitchen was awash in the morning light, warm and homey, smelling of baked bread and bacon. Breakfast was over ten minutes ago, but Bob had lingered. Ida looked at her tall, lean son, a high school football player, looking so much like his father. Soon he'd be gone to Purdue. He stood awkwardly, finally helped himself to another slice of thick white bread with last summer's strawberry jam, the chunks of berries red and still sweet and somewhat firm. Then he said something that caught Ida off guard.

"What?" she said more sharply than she had meant to.

"I said," Bob hesitated slightly. "I've been thinking...maybe I should put off college."

"What do you mean 'put off'?"

"We just can't swing it right now, Mama. Maybe I can go next year. Purdue will still be there," Bob said, his voice intense.

"Don't be silly," Ida objected. "You know we will help with the cost as much as possible. We will work it out," she said, her high hopes for him not yet gone. "You'll stay with Helen and Henry in Lafayette and get a part-time job somewhere down there. And if you do well, the school will reissue your scholarship."

"Mama, listen. They didn't take away the scholarship because I didn't do well. A lot of people are going to school after losing jobs and many can't pay their own way. The school has less money and so someone loses out. I guess, this time, it's me. And you heard Helen. Henry has taken a cut in pay from the church, so she wants me to pay rent. And with Papa still looking and me not working, there just isn't the money this year." His tone and eyes were pleading.

They stood a while in silence. Outside a rooster crowed, and the morning train whistled its lonely wail.

"But what will you do here?" Ida's voice broke just a bit as she turned back to the breakfast dishes. "There are no jobs here and no schooling to be had."

"I will find work." Bob said this with such conviction, Ida had to smile. Ah, the buoyancy of youth. "In the meantime, I will build Uncle Herman's garage."

"Well, it's kind of Herman to provide work, but it isn't engineering, is it?"

He shook his head; Ida was unclear on whether it meant he agreed or disagreed.

"Tell you what," he said. "I'll fix up the back porch for a bedroom — "

"There's no heat out there," she interrupted, her voice rising from disappointment.

"I know, but summer's coming!" Talking fast. "And there are blankets. If I fix up the back porch, you will have an empty room upstairs that you can rent out. And I'll keep looking while I work with Uncle Herman. I'll find something. In the meantime, you'll have some money in case I have trouble finding a job right away."

He waited. Her hands moved without thought, washing then rinsing each dish in water heated on the stovetop. She heard the constant drip of the icebox ice melting. She'd have to check it when the dishes were finished. She breathed a long, deep sigh. The energy to fight him flowed out of her into the hot soapy water. His plan was a good one; he had thought it through. She stopped, having run out of dishes, hands soaking in the warmth. With a head shake, she reached for a towel and turned to him. "John Robert, I swear, if you don't get an education, I will be sorely disappointed."

"I know."

"But..." She raised a still-wet spatula to emphasize her words, then dropped her hand, deflated. "I suppose you are right about the money. Everyone is short these days...you, us, Helen and Henry, the school... everyone except Uncle Herman. The Doerings have always been penny pinchers."

Thursday, October 2, 1930
LaSalle County TB Sanitarium
Ottawa, Illinois

Dear Brother Henry and Sister Helen,

I'm truly ashamed of myself for not writing sooner but I know you will forgive.

Things have been going along very slowly lately sometimes it seems to me like they were in reverse. This past week has been a bad one as food and I do not agree; just the smell of it makes me sick. I think perhaps this is due to a test that was given me ten days ago. It was an intravenous they shoot into the arm (about ½ glass full) and when this serum hits the kidneys or affected parts they turn opaque and show exactly how badly you are affected, that is the X-rays show it, and while this serum is still in the system it causes disorders.

Well two of my girls have had birthdays within the past ten days, I hope that next year I will be able to celebrate with them.

Next Sunday is communion Sunday and I don't expect any company although I know Mame would like to come.

I want to thank you so much for the prayer book you sent me. I read it every day and wish I had when I was with my family. This book should be in every Christian home.

Must close for now but will try to do better later.

From your Bro. Pete

Peter's weak hand rose like a beacon and motioned Ida to the bed. His voice had become harsh, little more than a whisper at times, his breath running out long before a full sentence could be spoken.

"Sit with me. For a while," he said.

Ida sat down on the wooden chair at bedside. John had driven her and Mame down to "talk some sense into Pete," as Mame put it, and now the two of them were off talking to some administrator, leaving her alone with Peter. He wanted to come home; his parents and sister Mary were making plans to bring him back to the farm soon. His brother Ras was also in agreement. "Ottawa is just so far away. Pete would do better with more visitors," he claimed.

"Am I...making a...mistake...wanting to coming home?" Peter gasped.

Ida looked at the shell of the man she had known. His sandy hair was dry and straw-like, sticking up in shocks from so many hours in bed, his bright blue eyes, now sunken and faded to a dull gray. His face was as white as the paper birch outside the screen wall. Several blankets cocooned his body to protect from the cool autumn breeze on his porch bedroom. So thin! she thought.

"I want...to be closer...to...the children...and Mame," he managed.

She had been told that he wasn't eating well and hadn't felt good at all the last few weeks, but she wasn't ready for this transformation. Maybe it was time for him to come home. Being surrounded by loved ones might be good for his mind, even if it did nothing to stop the progress of the disease.

"I don't want...to die...here...alone," he said, through tears.

"No, Peter, I don't think you are making a mistake," Ida answered. She took his hand in hers, felt the dry skin stretched across the bones. Once a strong working farmer's hand, now skeletal.

"If you come home, you'll get to know your children again," Ida said, venturing toward a happier ending. "We just took Bobby out to the farm for a couple weeks stay." Ida smiled, shaking her head slightly. "He never stops moving, and so, neither do I. He is such a busy laddie, and I am always glad to share his energy with his other grandma. I suppose Mame told you, but he's talking quite a bit now, and is a real mischief-maker even when he's trying to be good."

Pete smiled and nodded.

"And little Maryon is such a jewel. She worries about everyone else in the world: me, her mother, you, her Aunt Mary — she is very fond of Mary. And of course, her farm grandma and grandpa. Most of her talk is about making sure other people are OK."

"Sweet...girl," Pete whispered.

"Did Papa tell you that he and Bob are building a garage for Herman Doering? I said, 'Fine, do it!' Anything to keep them out from under foot!"

Peter started to laugh, but it quickly turned into a wet, spine-chilling cough. He covered his mouth with an old towel, which — based on the yellow and pink spots that soiled it throughout — had been used for this purpose many times. Startled, Ida stood up, backed away, and covered her own nose and mouth with her omnipresent hankie. Peter, perhaps seeing the fear in her eyes, motioned her to a nearby sink to wash her hands as his coughing subsided.

"I can't...laugh...anymore," he finally whispered with a gentle smile.

Ida, having washed all remnants of disease away, she hoped, turned her kind eyes on him again. "Come home, Peter."

Tuesday, October 28, 1930
Woodstock, Illinois

Dear Helen,

I suppose you think I have been overcome by the heat or something but I'm still able to be up and around and at work every day at Wiem's Store.

Bobby is back home again after two weeks on the farm where he was "so good." Of course, he was like no one but Pete. "Pete was always so good, so perfect when he was a baby." But he is still the squally, spunky, sassy little mutt as before now that he's back. It must be our influence!

And has Mama told you that Pete is coming home? I don't know whether I'm glad or sorry—I keep thinking about how much worse off he was last year at home—and at first I put down my foot & told him to stay—but he gets so homesick and he can't get well that way and his mother and Mary both encourage & insist that if he wants to come home he should. I wonder if it's really because they think he'll be better off or because Mary doesn't like to make the trip to Ottawa. I told Pete I was afraid to let him come, but they built a new porch for him & "maybe" he can have all the fresh air he needs tho he'll have to fight for every inch of "draft" & I will let him take the chance but if he gets worse instead of better back he goes even if we have to pay our own way. Ras writes to him all the time telling him to be satisfied & goes down every 6 weeks or two months to keep him satisfied. If he made as many trips as Mary and Papa, Pete wouldn't get so lonesome and discouraged. But talk is easier. Mary has been intending to make the trip down to get Pete & Pete wants me along so when I gave her the word that he wanted to come next weekend she decided she couldn't go Sunday but would go Saturday & in the same breath said, "Of course you can't go on Saturday so I'll take Andy Larsen along to drive so I can be with Pete." I don't know what Pete will do about that because he wants me—but maybe he'll be glad enough to get home so he won't care. If Peter's throat doesn't get along so good I'm going to get Aunt Fanny's Ray Machine or else buy one so he can have the rays. Mary thought it was all foolish to want to give him Rays but maybe she'll change her mind if he starts dying by inches while she watches. I, for one, want him to get well if I have to fight the whole country to prove it.

I must have a grouch on today seems like everything I say is mean.

*I'll try & write nice things next time because there's lots of them,
too—I guess more than the bad ones—but I picked the wrong day.
Must close now.*

Lots of love to you and Henry,

Mame

"Oh, I just love these quiet Sunday afternoons!" Ida said, poking
at John to move over on the davenport. "A good time to do a little
crocheting!"

"Hmph." John scooted over with sleepy eyes. "A good time to take
a nap."

"Didn't you think Thanksgiving turned out well? That turkey you
got was quite good and now the children can't say they cannot
remember ever having turkey. How much did you pay for that bird?"

John sat up a little straighter, readying himself for a conversation
instead of a nap, while preferring the latter. "Cost? Nothing."

Ida looked at him, incredulous, hands stopping mid-stitch.

"I traded that extra wood out back for it...and a chicken for
Christmas. Don't need the wood since we are on coal now. It was
starting to rot so I think we got a great deal. You know what the Elks
charged for Thanksgiving turkey dinner this year? $1.50 a plate! See
how much I saved you?"

"Why Papa, that's the longest speech I've heard from you in a long
time." They both chuckled.

"I'm so glad all the young people went out to the farm to see Peter
today," she said. "It's nice and quiet here. Pete was surely happy to be
home, wasn't he? I could almost see color in his cheeks."

Ida's hands lapsed into the monotony of the crochet hook sliding
through loops and being pulled evenly back.

"Yes, I think we'll see ups and downs, like Tuesday when he was so
sick he just sent everyone away..."

"And on Ma Rasmussen's birthday, too." She finished the thought
for him, eyes on her work. "Didn't Mame say he had a temperature of

104? But then on Friday he was better."

"Ups and downs." John nodded sagely.

"And yesterday was very nice...a holiday visit to Moncur's Greenhouse. Could you believe all that color. The Chrysanthemums were gorgeous!"

"Should have got one," he said, the nice husband.

"Don't worry, Papa." She patted his knee. "I love my begonia, and I plan on having color from it all winter and replanting it in the spring."

"Did you see Bobby in church this morning?" Ida changed the subject.

"Now what?" he asked, his expression anticipating trouble.

"While Reverand Koffmann was preaching, Bobby stood in the pew and imitated his every move. I think we have a minister in the making. And Maryon just loves to go to Sunday School. You know what she said to me yesterday?" Ida asked.

"What?"

"'Grandma, are you tired? Then why don't you rest.' Isn't that cute. She's going to be a nurse or a teacher. Mark my words."

"Or a mother," he said smiling at the woman he had loved for many years.

Thursday, December 4, 1930
Woodstock, Illinois

Dear Helen and Henry:

Everything is quiet along the Potomac this evening. Father and I are all alone so that means a good time for letters.

Bob is out with the boys. Ed is with Dorothy and Mame & children are at Ras's. Bob and Edna went to the farm to get her just before supper. They took the children, too and on the way home they stopped at Ras's. Peter had rather a bad spell, so Edna said. Maybe too much company today. That is always hard for him because he is so weak.

He is able to eat a little more since he came home. He eats in *a reclining position because sitting up to eat nauseates him. The poor man, he surely doesn't show any gain. It appears to me as though he gets weaker. And Mame seems to think that sometime in the future he is going to be well again.*

All are well at this writing and surely hope you are both in good health. Little Maryon was telephoning the other day and this is what I overheard her saying, "Hello Jesus, will you send my daddy home to me — please send him because I like him."

A few days before that she came to me and said "I was talking to my daddy, Grandma." You did, I said, and what did your daddy say? "Well he said 'Hello Maryon and hello Bobby and Grandma.' Daddy said he was sick. He said he was awful sick." I tried to say he wasn't but she insisted he was sick. She can't understand that if daddy is well why he can't come live with her.

This won't go until tomorrow due to the late hour.

Love to you both – Mother

When Peter had come home in early November, after spending eight months at the sanitarium, he was but a shadow of the brother that Ras had known. Peter had lain on that sun-porch cot for just over a month, when one morning Mary came in carrying his breakfast and found him with his long thin fingers laid across his eyes, as if shutting out the morning sun. Now Ras lifted the coffin with the seven other men. It was a light load.

Ras remembered the day he took the photo that had been placed beneath Pete's hands in the coffin. Ras had focused his camera, smiling at the image of his one-year-old niece in the viewfinder. Clad in overalls, Maryon Petrea was chubby and robust much like her mother Mame who was more than six months pregnant and much unlike her father, Peter, who, Ras noticed, looked tired and thin. Pete had spoken that day of a shoulder injury two years earlier that left his arms and hands too painful to move.

"Some days my fingers are too stiff to milk the cows," he said.

"Takes me hours. Mame does more milking than I do sometimes. But then it passes."

What they didn't know in 1928 when the picture was taken — what no one knew — was that their sister Mary was also infected, carrying her ex-husband's tuberculosis back with her from the southwest and infecting Pete with a kiss or a shared spoon. But Mary would be alright, Ras thought hopefully. She was only a carrier without symptoms. He would not countenance losing both brother and sister to consumption.

Sunday, December 28, 1930
Woodstock, Illinois

Dear Helen & Henry:

Everyone is feeling better here at home. Christmas day Bob was sick in bed all day. He felt so wretched Christmas Eve that he couldn't even open his gift boxes. Edna had been sick for several days before. Marion's vaccination didn't seem to bother so much but she had a bad cold, enough to stay in bed.

Little Maryon's whooping cough is slightly easier now. While the others were all feeling so ill she was having such severe coughing spells, choking and vomiting. So between them all, I had not such a pleasant time. My cold was over with, so at least I had that to be thankful for.

Bobby does not cough very hard as yet. Am of the opinion that his will not be as severe. And he is a nice little chap. He can go visit Aunt Helen and Uncle Henry now because he keeps his bed all nice and dry and his little suits day times. And he talks so cute. In fact he is a general favorite around here.

We received the Christmas box Wednesday and everything was so nice and we all say "Thank you" most heartily. The cookies were so good, we still have most of the dark ones because I knew they would keep and no one felt like eating before. We are beginning to have appetites again.

Edna gave me the usual $12.00 Christmas savings. Bob a box *of stationary and Mame a Nellie Don apron and a linen table cloth. Dorothy gave me two hankies. Wasn't everyone good to me?*

Thank you for the underwear for Bob. These are so good he can still get much wear out of them, but what is Henry wearing?

Mame had such a lovely letter from Louise Thomas, and I had such a sweet card — "To my friend's Mother."

Mrs. Thomas has been so nice to me since Peter was so bad and during the time of his passing away.

I started this letter this afternoon and wanted to get it mailed tonight — now I just happened to think that the train goes an hour earlier on Sunday night so you won't get this until Tuesday. I'm so sorry.

Well good-night dear hearts. A happy and healthy New Year to you both.

Love from all, Mother

Ida folded the letter and put it into an envelope. Mame and the children would stay here now that Pete was gone. Not the way she had imagined her golden years, but still in these difficult times, having everyone gathered under one roof was not a bad thing. And who knew what the New Year would bring. Peace and Prosperity, Ida thought, smiling. She licked the flap and sealed 1930 into the past.

GLORIA T. DIFULVIO is a writer of (mostly) creative nonfiction who views storytelling as a tool for personal and community change. By day, she is a public health academic with a special interest in the role of personal narratives and health. She uses participatory community methods such as digital storytelling, documentary film, and photovoice to deepen our understanding of health. You can find her nonfiction in such publications as *Huffington Post, Ravishly, Crossing Genres,* and *DaCunha,* where she currently serves as an editor of nonfiction. She lives in Hadley, Massachusetts, with her wife, Australian Shepherd, and two cats. Visit her website at gloriadifulvio.com.

This piece is a story about the ways in which our family history shapes us long before we may be born. The story, about my father's early life, is based on family genealogical records passed on to me by an uncle, data from the 1920 census which shows my grandfather living without his children with an aunt and her family, and oral history from my father. I have incorporated my grandmother's death from the Spanish Flu (Flu of 1918) as the central event that changed not only my father's life, but the generations to follow.

BY GLORIA DIFULVIO

If She Had Lived

The story is she was hanging up clothes when the aches and pains crept into her body. It was an unusually warm day, but she began to feel chilled — as if winter days had snuck into August. She felt weakness in her knees, started to sweat. She saw her neighbor working in her garden and called for her. Could she help her inside? Perhaps watch her three small children? Before she could take her first step towards the door, she collapsed, the morning's labor of laundry now lying before her in the dusty grass.

Her neighbor was afraid. She took her arm, helped her up, and walked her slowly inside. She undressed her and placed a cool cloth on her forehead. She shuffled the kids outside, asking the oldest, only five years old, to watch the younger ones. She hoped she got them out of the house in time. She wanted to stay and care for her but knew she would only endanger herself. This flu left few survivors in its wake.

She lay in bed for three days, fever burning through her body. She wanted nothing more than to embrace her youngest son, held to her breast for barely a year. But she also knew she needed to protect him as his little body wouldn't survive this virus. She heard him cry out for her from the neighbors' window, each cry sending a shiver down her spine. "I will come for you, my baby boy," she whispered as she took her last breath.

My grandmother, Umilta DiFulvio, died from the flu in 1918, nearly fifty years before I was born. Her death was sudden and sparked a turn of events in my father's life that profoundly changed him. I have always felt a curious kinship for this virus — like a dysfunctional family member you need to embrace because he is a part of your being. Not unlike my father, I often wondered how life might be different had she survived.

I imagine my father as a one-year-old, crying for those three days, searching for the warm breast of his mother. I imagine him wondering why she had abandoned him. I imagine him yearning for her embrace, which until this moment kept him safe and warm. I imagine him alone, with a hunger in his belly and a longing for a touch that would console him. If she had lived, she would have scooped him into her arms once the fever broke, held him close and reassured him of her love. She would have rocked him to sleep while he closed his eyes, tiny hands clinging to her dress.

If she had lived, my grandfather would have kept his mason's job, laying bricks to build the city's center. He used to labor knowing that the woman he loved so much would care for his children while he was away. He would welcome the ache in his back at the end of a brutal day because it meant he could feed his family. Instead, when the demand of caring for his children made him late for the work lines, they hired another immigrant to replace him. He continued to show up, desperate for a day's pay, only to return home with empty pockets.

If she had lived, my grandfather's despair would have subsided once she touched his face, her fingertips telling him she would stay by his side. Instead, he woke up to a tear-stained pillow, wondering why she was crying, only to find the tears were his own.

If she had lived, my grandfather wouldn't have said to the nuns at the orphanage, "It's just for awhile, until I find work. No, they cannot go up for adoption. I will be back for them." His three children wouldn't have cried at the entrance, with their arms outstretched, reaching for the remnants of the life they knew — if only briefly. My father, barely a toddler, would not have lain weeping, alone in his crib —

thinking his mother would come for him, soon, soon—while the nuns attended to their many charges.

Instead, he learned the only way to ease his suffering was to withdraw deeply into himself, even though he might never find his way out. At night, when my father was lonely and afraid, he closed his eyes tight, hoping the bully would forget where he slept—terror paralyzing his body. His heart hardened with each passing day so that after nearly ten years inside those walls, he could barely feel its beat.

The day his father and new wife were to return, he was filled with anticipation. He took his siblings' hands and waited outside for the family that would save him. If she had lived, his excitement wouldn't have crumbled when he realized his father was not the man he remembered and his new mother was a stranger.

If she had lived, my father would not have carefully crafted the walls that barricaded his heart from the world. He would have felt he was worthy, would have fallen in love. Instead, my father walked through life as a solitary man. A gifted athlete, he never pursued his dream of baseball because he never believed he could. He drove aimlessly across the country seeking solace in his religion and searching for his purpose. He traveled to Italy and brought home a wife he barely knew. He spent the next thirty years wondering why his marriage still left him empty and alone.

If my grandmother had lived, I would have known a different man.

I imagine a father more involved, feeling he belonged in the family he created. Instead, he lurked in the shadows, unsure of how to walk in his own shoes, in his own home.

Instead of a withdrawn and broken man, he would have stood tall and confident. He would have accepted the missteps of his children with an empathetic, firm hand rather than a punishing one. His anger would have been more predictable. He wouldn't have looked to his children for his happiness but would have found it within himself.

My father longed for his mother until his death at age seventy-one. The night before he died, he told me he saw her—she was waiting for him — a smile on her face. He wanted nothing more than finally to feel her arms around him again.

Nearly one hundred years after the flu crept into my grandmother's body and took her life, I wonder what my father would have been like, if his eyes would have reflected contentment with his present rather than a yearning for his past.

If she had lived.

JULIA GIMBEL has been lucky to experience a host of different careers over the years — from store planner, to fitness instructor, to jewelry designer, to volunteer — all while keeping the family peace. She lives in Whitefish Bay, Wisconsin, with her husband, Josh, and their two young adults, Lena and Elijah, in a home where the entire family dotes on the pugs. Thirty years after earning her Bachelor of Science in Journalism from the University of Wisconsin-Madison, she finally has time to sit down and write.

Long ago, my late mother created a scrapbook containing letters, pictures, and memorabilia that my Dad sent to her while he served in the South Pacific during World War II. Several years ago, while showing this book to my daughter, I discovered a sixty-page, hand-written journal tucked inside the back flap. Apparently, after he retired, Dad spent many cold winter afternoons in his study, filling sheet after sheet of lined notebook paper with his recollections of the war. He didn't talk about the war much, but clearly he had a lot to say.

Dad has been gone for years now, but as I read his journal I can hear his voice as if he is in the room telling me these stories himself. His writing is funny, opinionated, and full of details. The scrapbook and journal together create a vivid picture of one young man's experiences after leaving home for the Navy in July 1943.

Seventy odd years later, I am compelled to help Dad tell his story, and the stories of so many like him who are long gone. I find myself retracing his steps, filling in the blanks with my own research, interviewing veterans, and fleshing out the details to provide the reader with a window into what life was like during that long ago war.

BY JULIA GIMBEL

In a Sailor's Footsteps

My nephew, Pat Morgan, possesses a worn, black leather scrapbook that has been in our family since World War II. A portrait of Dad in his newly earned Ensign's stripe and star anchors the cover—the leather beautifully tooled with intricate swirls, softened and cracked over the years from its travels from home to home. Inside, the worn pages are filled with hundreds of photos, scraps of paper, letters, and other memorabilia that Dad sent home to Mom during the war.

I was aware that the scrapbook existed while I was growing up—all five of us kids pulled it out of the dresser drawer and took turns paging through it. But recently I was surprised to find a sixty-page, handwritten journal that my father had tucked inside the back cover. Even more startling was how it would go on to change the focus of my life.

I brought the book home to show to my daughter, Lena, thinking it would help her complete a high school history research assignment; I hoped the things my parents saved might inspire her and interest her classmates. What I didn't anticipate was that seeing the book again and hearing the words of my late father would take me on a trip of my own—retracing his steps, enjoying his sense of humor, learning more about the war, and, finally, sharing his experiences with others.

Dad never talked much about the war, and obviously he survived or I wouldn't be here to tell his story. But when I read his journal, I realized that as he first sat down during his retirement to log his memories, he was driven by the need to make a permanent record of everything he had never said out loud.

In the weeks after Lena turned in her assignment, I couldn't get Dad's voice out of my head — his stories darting into my thoughts at odd moments. Was the journal his way of telling me now that we should have talked more when he was alive? During the last decade of his life, he could have answered so many questions for me, but I was wrapped up in and distracted by my own young family at the time.

Maybe his words consumed me because my son, Elijah, is now the same age as Dad was when the Japanese bombed Pearl Harbor in December 1941 and set in motion everything that would happen to my father in the following four years. Elijah packing his possessions and moving into his first dorm room differed so greatly from my father packing his things and heading off to war. Both experiences, though, suggested adventure to a young man who had rarely been away from home.

What was it like for Dad? I've asked myself that question a million times since I first read and then transcribed his journal. I wondered if his heart was pounding as he walked into the Navy recruitment office to enlist during his summer break from the University of Wisconsin–Madison in July 1942. I wanted to jump in the pool with him as he learned to swim during his time at Notre Dame in the V-12 program. He marched past Grant's Tomb in New York City for two months before realizing it was even there — a Midshipman in training at Columbia University, too scared to avert his eyes to the left. I wanted to walk with my father, no longer a carefree college student, as he marched with his peers in strict formation, learning the ways of the Navy.

Since my father is gone, I've let the words in his journal lead my research. An introvert at heart, I've had to reach out to strangers for help in piecing together and understanding the things Dad went through. From veterans willing to share their own stories, to Honor Flight staff, to history professors and World War II newsletter editors — these people filled in the gaps for me and enthusiastically encouraged me in my efforts to tell Dad's story.

My dad, Robert Thomas McCurdy, was part of the very first wave of young men selected for the Navy's new officer training program. On July 1, 1943, he reported to Notre Dame to begin four months of Navy indoctrination called V-12 (for no reason other than to give it a designation). He continued on to Midshipmen school (V-7) in New York City, where after ninety days he was officially an officer in the Navy. Soon he was on his way to the South Pacific.

After a week's leave in Freeport, Illinois, I headed west for San Francisco to report to a landing craft unit. The train left Chicago at 7:00 pm on Sunday and arrived in San Francisco around noon the following Wednesday. It's hard to believe that this is maybe a four-hour flight nowadays. I remember when I kissed Mom goodbye. It was always very, very hard to do, saying goodbye that is. There were a lot of goodbyes in those days – many of them were, of course, forever.

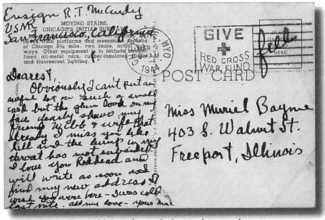

Posted by author's father to her mother,
just before boarding his transport overseas

At the dock in San Francisco on February 11, 1944, Dad joined a sea of over one thousand other men, all dressed in white or navy blue, pouring onto the gangways to climb aboard the USS *Ommaney Bay* — the ship that would deliver them to their assignments in the South Pacific. Each sailor balanced a heavy canvas sea bag awkwardly over his shoulder, freshly stenciled with his name and containing all his worldly possessions. His uniforms, sleeping gear, and towels were tightly rolled inside in a specific order, drilled into his memory through repeated practice of packing and unpacking the bag. Additionally, for the enlisted men, a hammock and mattress were wrapped around the exterior of the bag and bound fast with a line.

Dad didn't need the hammock because, as an officer, he wouldn't be sleeping with the masses. "Rank has its privileges," he'd written in his journals.

I sailed out of San Francisco on a brand new light aircraft carrier named the USS Ommaney Bay. The food and service were excellent. There were some ground swells right outside of San Francisco that caused the first bout of seasickness and then we ran into a vicious storm that lasted four days. As a passenger officer I shared quarters with another young Ensign. He was seasick for at least a week. Being seasick is a good way to lose weight.

Millions of troops, sailors, and officers serving in World War II traveled to their assignments on troop transport ships of one kind or another. During the war, the Navy leased and converted many civilian ocean liners, Liberty ships, and smaller vessels just for this purpose. Even the famous ocean liner RMS *Queen Mary* was stripped of its elaborate décor, painted gray, armored, and put into service carrying up to an astounding fifteen thousand troops per ocean crossing.

Dad was aboard a ship with a Navy designation of "CVE Escort Carrier," but these ships were often casually called "baby flattops."

They were about half the length of the regular fleet aircraft carriers and held far fewer aircraft — only about twenty-eight to the larger ships' seventy or so. Still these ships were HUGE, almost two football fields in length. His ship, the USS *Ommaney Bay* CVE 79, packed with passengers (like Dad), troops, supplies, and aircraft, made its maiden voyage, bound for Brisbane, Australia, where the men would go on to find their permanent assignments.

> *There were 50 passenger officers and for the first week only 5 or 6 of us showed up for meals. I had never been able to endure carnival rides so I was quite proud that in my whole career at sea – mostly on small craft, I never once was sick.*
>
> *There were about 1000 enlisted men passengers on board. They were cooped up in the well deck – like the hold of the ship. I strolled down there one day and discovered that 1000 men can create one monstrous amount of vomit. Shower facilities were also very limited for the young sailors. Needless to say, they were not traveling first class. There was no air conditioning on the ship.*

My father wasn't kidding when he said the personal hygiene options for the sailors were lacking. The only showers were salt water, and the little brick of soap produced no lather at all. Once the saltwater dried, the men must have felt even dirtier than before the shower.

As I researched more about what it was like to "ship out," one veteran I met, Al Exner, told me he had never been on a boat or ship at all during his training at Great Lakes after joining the Navy at age seventeen. His transfer ship was a converted ocean liner, and he joined seven thousand other men the day they headed to England. He recalled for me the conditions in the hold of his ship:

> On the ship, the quarters were very tight. There were fabric pieces stretched onto pipes to act as beds, and these were

stacked four high. There was only about 18 inches between each canvas. The fellow above me was very heavy, and if I didn't get into my bunk before him, I would have to squeeze into the small space left below from his weight sagging the canvas.

The narrow aisle between the bunks contained a jumble of sea bags, so the men were forced to clamber over everything to get to and from their beds. The sailors' quarters were below the waterline, with no portholes, the air thick and hot for the men crowded into those confined spaces.

Much slower and barely armored CVEs, like Dad's, were cheap and quick to build and soon filled a gap in the Navy's fleet. Archivist and historian Lincoln Cushing notes that these ships were also spoken of sarcastically as "Combustible, Vulnerable, and Expendable" because of all of the qualities that made them less than ideal in wartime.

The Ommaney Bay was probably ill fated from the start. It was on its maiden voyage and the crew, as well as the officers were having difficulty adapting to life at sea. The Navy didn't have the "practice" option in 1943. They went right to work — on-the-job training — just as we did on our LCT's (Landing Craft–Tanks).

At night we traveled under blackout conditions and of course, were on a zigzag path to make it more difficult for submarines to aim their torpedoes. One night all hell broke loose, we came to a dead stop, sirens blaring, lifeboats were lowered and every searchlight on board turned on. At this point we would have been a prime target for any Japanese submarine nearby. A harried muster (roll count) had indicated that one of the passenger sailors was missing (man overboard). The search continued for several hours and then was abandoned. The missing sailor happily was found — in one of the lifeboats. He had thought it would be fun to join the search.

The Captain was obviously a humanitarian and did what his heart dictated. I would think his naval superiors would have thought differently — endangering perhaps 2000 men to rescue one chap.

These new members of the Navy were very young and inexperienced. A practical joke by one young sailor could have forever changed (or ended) the lives of everyone on board.

The ship must have been beautiful in its own way — not a rusty spot in sight as it headed off to war. The sick bay, or dressing station, was the medical area set up to treat those wounded in battle. Men could be treated for almost any injury up to and including minor surgery. It contained twenty-five to thirty bunks and medical supplies stored in lockers.

We couldn't get over how well the ship was equipped. It had a beautiful sick bay, at least one M.D. and the usual assistants. One of the ensigns who was right out of dental school looked longingly at the equipment. He was also a passenger. I heard the two ships' company dentists complaining about having to spend the next 18 months doing amalgam-silver fillings. They were "gold crown" type chaps.

On some ships, like the USS Suwannee, the sick bay was also ordinarily used as the ship's barbershop, complete with several barber chairs. Al Exner was a Navy Medical Technician, and he said that he often slept in the dressing station on his ship in order to escape the suffocating conditions in the bunks below deck.

Deck space was at a premium as sailors clad in lifejackets sprawled about just to get some sunshine and fresh air. Men could stretch their legs exploring the ship or join one of the card games that quickly sprang up. Training exercises and daily inspections continued for everyone. On larger transport ships, the crew produced daily newsletters with news of the world gathered from the radio. Some vessels even had entertainment, such as movies and shows, put on by Special Services.

*We had a lot of time to kill enroute. I believe it took us 16 or 17
days to reach Brisbane, Australia. There was a ship's library and
books to read however.*

Surprisingly, many ships the size of the one Dad was aboard had
a snack bar, called a "gedunk." No one is one hundred percent sure
where the term "gedunk" came from, but one theory is that it came
from a popular newspaper comic strip called "Harold Teen" that had
called ice cream "gedunk" ever since the 1920s. Over the years, the
term spread from ice cream to snacks and candy, and finally extended
to the actual place on board where sailors could purchase these items,
as well as cigarettes, when the mess was closed.

Speaking of the mess hall, feeding the troops was a major daily
undertaking. On a typical transport ship, the sailors would often
have to line up for several hours to get their chow. One sailor wrote a
piece about getting into the mess hall, having food dumped onto his
tray, and moving along a chest high table, eating as he went. When
he reached the end of the table, he washed his tray and left the mess
hall, only to repeat this process later for the second meal of the day.
Al Exner remembers this compartment on his ship was large enough
to feed several hundred men at once. Officers were served their meals
in their own quarters or in officer dining rooms.

In the seventeen days it took Dad to reach Brisbane, he and the
other officers got to know each other and filled their time prowling
the ship and carrying on just as the enlisted sailors did. However, this
voyage for young Ensign McCurdy was not entirely smooth sailing.

*It was on the Ommaney Bay that I realized I was never going to be
the gung ho type guy with dangerous weapons. The ship's gunnery
officer offered to conduct some target practice off the stern of the
ship — we being the shooters. I took my trusty 45, aimed carefully at some floating cans and then shot just once. The noise was
deafening so in a daze I turned toward the instructor pointing the*

weapon directly at his stomach asking him casually "What do I do now?" He quickly turned my hand away uttering some unkind profanities and that was the end of target practice. I could very easily have killed him and to this day have never fired another weapon — in vain or otherwise.

Clearly, the Navy officer's training Dad underwent had not dwelt on how to use their personal weapons. Unbelievably, he (and probably so many others) went off to war without even knowing how to use his own gun, which he was given when he left the service.

According to family legend, a few years later Dad brought the gun out of storage, placing it on the kitchen table to show a neighbor. My oldest sister and brother remember this vividly because my mother read Dad the riot act. She wanted him to get rid of it at once! So, just like that, the neighbor became the proud new owner of a Navy-issued pistol. Dad once mentioned this to me, wondering whatever had become of his "gift."

If you're a history buff, it's hard to resist following every interesting avenue that appears as you research. So, of course I was curious about what happened to the USS *Ommaney Bay*. First, it was sent on to Pearl Harbor for use as a training vessel. From there, it sailed to the Philippines to provide air cover for what is widely considered the fiercest Navy battle of the war — the Battle of Leyte Gulf. The USS *Ommaney Bay* helped sink one Japanese cruiser and played a role in crippling many other enemy vessels. The Japanese Navy never recovered from this battle.

A kamikaze later sealed the fate of the USS *Ommaney Bay* on January 4, 1945, in the Sulu Seas in the Surigao Strait. This beautiful new ship that Dad took when he left the United States for Australia was struck on the starboard side, right through the flight deck and into the fully fueled planes stored below. There was no power or water to control the intense fires that erupted, and when they began to spread toward the ship's torpedo storage, the captain ordered all to abandon ship.

A nearby destroyer, the USS Burns, later launched a torpedo and scuttled the ship, destroying it so the enemy couldn't salvage any part of it. Of the original crew of over one thousand men, ninety-three were killed from the attack and resulting fires; scores more were wounded.

A film clip of the kamikaze attack on the *Ommaney Bay* shows the Japanese plane elude frantic anti-aircraft fire from the CVE's deck, then crash into the ship. Billows of thick, black smoke erupt.

It was chilling to see this piece of history, knowing that Dad traveled aboard this fine vessel and remembered it so vividly. There was so much pure luck involved — my father returned from the war unscathed while others, including members of the crew he traveled with on that ship, met their fates. My father likely was aware of what later happened to that ship, since his first journal entry about it mentions that it was "ill-fated from the start."

Dad stepped off that ship onto dry land where he spent a week before moving closer to his final destination.

Author's father in Brisbane

*We landed in Brisbane (that's in Australia, land of emeralds) and...
while waiting to 'ship out' we visited a lovely seaside cottage type
place. It was run by an English woman who referred to herself as
Lady Coot. We romped in the sand and surf and in general had lots
of fun. I was able to use my new swimming skills having learned the
art at South Bend.*

*We played a lot of black jack to kill time and Jack Forgeson really
cleaned us out. Eventually he confessed that he had been a part-time
black jack dealer in Reno, Nevada during the summers while in college.
I never saw him again either. He was a real nice chap.*

Dad, however, was off to find the Skipper of the little ship he would
call home — LCT 977.

*We sailed on a smaller vessel up north and west to Milne Bay in
Southern New Guinea. All I can remember is that we slept on deck —
fortunately it did not rain. Our voyage was along the Great Barrier
Reef that I understand is quite an attraction — for tourists — at 22,
who cares?*

At twenty-two, Elijah will be leaving college and entering a world
full of opportunities where he will get to choose his own destiny. For
Dad in 1942, the only choice he got to make was to join the Navy or
end up being drafted into the Army. He was swept up in one of the
most tumultuous times our country has ever experienced. His return
home after the war was not a given, and for three years all he had
wanted was to come home safely, marry the girl of his dreams, and get
on with the rest of his life.

And yet, there is a spirit of adventure in these passages in Dad's
journal. Here was a young man, who had barely left his small hometown
in Illinois, suddenly traveling all over the South Pacific. He met some
fantastic (and some nefarious) people, survived near misses, incredible
boredom and tedious tasks, all while helping to lead a ship full of men at

such a tender age. The people he recalled and the stories he told in his journal are so vivid that I finally realize what an impact the war years had on him.

Little signs were always there. When I was twelve years old, our family went on a glass bottom boat ride while vacationing in Hawaii. Dad was the only one who could manage the swells of the ocean, walking across the deck as if he were on solid ground. I thought he was amazing at the time, and I still do.

I hate war stories and to this day have kept pretty mum about the services. In fact my son Bob was quite startled many years ago when he learned that I had spent "time" — in the Navy that is.

It is a remarkable sight to imagine: him tucked into his little office on those snowy winter afternoons in the early 2000s, scribbling in his journal about years spent in the tropical heat so long ago. He humbly focused on and delighted in our family's life, all the while quietly and persistently recording his thoughts and memories in that journal. I can still picture him sitting there in a V-neck sweater to ward off the chill, Miles Davis or John Lewis softly playing in the background, Siamese cat under the desk. He would tilt his head back to peer at me over his glasses as I walked in, offering me a grin. I always assumed he was just working numbers for his remaining accounting clients, but now I know he was pouring out his memories on sheet after sheet of notebook paper, a treasured testament for all who read them.

MYLES HOPPER writes creative nonfiction, and is the author of the forthcoming collection of stories, *The Color Red and Other Memories*. Elsewhere, he has written, "Memoir is my preferred way of trying to understand my possibly incomprehensible family of origin, including myself." He has a doctorate in cultural anthropology and a law degree, and has taught in several universities in the United States and the Canadian province of Newfoundland and Labrador. He also has consulted with nonprofits, and has been a board member of one which serves the families of gravely ill children, and another which serves homeless veterans and their families. Myles and his spouse live in Shorewood, Wisconsin, and they have two adult children. His website is myleshopper.com.

"Exodus Redux" is one of the linked stories in The Color Red. *By exploring universal themes, directly or indirectly, I endeavor to take the collection beyond the boundaries of my personal life experiences.*

When I decided to write memoir, I struggled to overcome my reluctance to include anything disparaging about certain people, living and dead, whom I love. Yet, I understood it was essential to resolve that struggle if the memoir were to be authentic. Thinking it might be useful to take a step or two away from my own reality to "see what happens," I drafted the opening story as fiction. What happened, in part, is my anthropology background came to the forefront in "The Teller," which presages much of the content of The Color Red. *A father in a Native North American tribe overcomes his reluctance to assume the role his people had expected of him: to be the one who tells the stories of the clan, as the young and old gather at the story fire. Writing about my alter ego made it easier to overcome my own reluctance, though his and mine do resurface on occasion.*

Preparing "Exodus Redux" for inclusion in Family Stories from the Attic *has allowed me to reexamine a significant transition that occurred in my young life. In doing so, I gained a deeper understanding of the words of the British author, Alan Bennett: " ... [Y]ou don't put yourself into what you write. You find yourself there."*

Exodus Redux

2016. Remembering Isaac.

"We were sacrificed."

"Yes," I said to my older brother. "Sacrificial lambs."

"Exactly."

1947. Genesis.

In the beginning of the 1947-48 school year, I attended a Jewish parochial school with a name that took forever to say: The Rabbi H. F. Epstein Hebrew Academy. Often shortened by omitting "Rabbi," the Academy was the first Jewish day school in Missouri, founded in 1943, the year of my birth. My two brothers — one three years older, the other four years younger — also attended the Academy. The older brother would complete grade school there, the younger brother would attend for only part of a kindergarten year, and I would attend from kindergarten through the fifth grade.

Each morning, we recited prayers and studied the *Torah*, other aspects of Judaism, and the Hebrew language. Each afternoon, we shifted to the standard Missouri school curriculum. My grades were good; there were teachers I liked; I had friends. I like to say their names: Doreen, Adele, Miriam, Benjie, Jeff, Harold, Ronnie, Joshua, and Karen.

A few names stand out to me. Ronnie was the friend I would hang out with on many weekends. Joshua's serious demeanor and penchant to give *Torah* lessons, from the first years of grade school, was befitting of what lay in store for him. Karen was the girl who always had my full attention, even when I wasn't with her. She had big brown eyes and shiny, dark brown hair she wore in bangs. I mean, I really loved Karen. On the school bus, I pulled her hair.

On balance, though, the Rabbi H. F. Epstein Hebrew Academy was a childhood experience that came with a cost too high for me to bear. What had begun as a vague feeling of resentment, by the third grade would begin to acquire significant clarity; each painful day I boarded a school bus headed for the Hebrew Academy was another day that marked me as *different*, an outsider. And a traumatic encounter with a school authority would intensify those feelings.

My family had moved to one of the units in a six-family apartment building that my maternal grandparents helped purchase. The building was across the street from a wonderful public school and its playground, one the neighborhood kids loved and I envied. They walked to school — some no farther than across the street — while I had to walk to the corner and wait for the school bus to take me somewhere I did not want to be taken.

Even though I had made friends with some of the kids, even though groups of us would hang out together, I never experienced the pleasure and the security that would have come from being their classmate: from truly being one of the gang. In my child's mind, the Rabbi H. F. Epstein Hebrew Academy itself kept me an outsider in my own neighborhood.

My parents' decision to send my brothers and me to that school occurred within historical context. My maternal grandparents had emigrated from Poland to America early in the twentieth century and had left behind many of their extended family members, a few of whom survived beyond the end of World War II. My father had been an American soldier in France and Germany when what was happening in the concentration camps became widely known. Following the Holocaust, Jews throughout the world, including my grandparents and parents, understood that sacrifices — financial and other — would be needed to ensure the future of Judaism and the Jewish people.

In spite of all of this, I don't believe my parents would have decided on their own that enrolling their children in a Jewish parochial school was essential to achieving that goal; there must have been considerable pressure from my mother's parents. My brothers and I did not want to be there; my parents, I believe, were ambivalent. But neither fact deterred four elders from continuing to send three boys as sacrifices on the altar of the Rabbi H. F. Epstein Hebrew Academy.

And so it was written. And so it came to pass.

In my own neighborhood, I was forlorn whenever I would watch the kids on their paved playground with painted lines for volleyball, kickball, basketball, football, softball, and hopscotch. Some of the students were Jewish, I knew, but they didn't have to wear a yarmulke and tzitzis (with its four corners under the shirt and knotted strings hanging outside). I wanted to be one of those kids. On many weekends and evenings, when the gates in the tall chain link fence that surrounded the playground were locked, kids would climb over and continue their games. I sometimes joined them, but those brief moments of camaraderie weren't enough to counter the painful reality of my isolation and loneliness. I often felt like a waif who wanders the streets of Old London at Christmas, his sooty face pressed against the outside of the candy store window.

The Rabbi H. F. Epstein Hebrew Academy didn't waste its limited budget on proper playgrounds. At its first location, there was a dirt play area. My classmates and I were little kids, at most in the third grade. We had no athletic equipment, other than some soccer-size rubber balls, and marble collections some of the boys brought from home in drawstring bags. We would scratch a circle in the dirt and kneel around it, as serious as men at an alley crap game. The only difference was we played with glass peewees and boulders.

The best thing the play area did have to offer was a treasure trove of rocks. We improvised. One otherwise normal day, about a dozen boys and a few girls lined up on two sides. I don't remember who it was that threw first, but when my rock hit my friend Harold high in the center of his forehead, blood flowed down his face and decorated his white shirt. We all froze. Everyone stared at Harold and his bloody face and shirt, and at me as I stared at Harold, while Harold just stared. Then, like a response to a starter's gun, we scattered. Trapped in a small, fenced playground far from our homes, I have no idea where we thought we might hide.

After murdering his brother Abel, Cain must have experienced a similar sense of panic. His dissembling before an omniscient God served only to make a bad situation worse. Unlike Abel, Harold lived. That's why he, though bleeding, could run into the school building.

I expected to hear, as did Cain, a thunderous voice emanating from nowhere and everywhere: "Who was it that endeavored to slay young Master Harold?" As I already predicted — *prophesied* would be more in keeping with the school's orientation — I was the only child blamed. Someone had ratted on me, or I had been frightened enough to confess my sin. Regardless, I was the child who had dispatched the rock on its true path, during an event that bore no resemblance whatsoever to the slaying of Goliath.

Someone old, like one of the Sanhedrin in the ancient Jerusalem temple, told me to report to the High Priest, cleverly disguised as the school Superintendent. Huge and intimidating, Rabbi Kuglowski led me to the basement.

Isaac must have felt something similar to my own trepidation when Abraham suggested they go for a little stroll up the mountain to offer a sacrifice. There was that moment when the son wondered aloud why the father had remembered the wood, fire, and knife, but had forgotten the lamb — at least the four-legged variety. As they ascended, perchance Isaac had trust in Abraham and was assured by his father's words of faith, "God will provide himself a lamb..." But as the Superintendent and I descended, following his less assuring "Come downstairs with me," I had no such trust. Certain there was no lamb in our basement or anywhere else in the building, I didn't have to wonder aloud whether I was in big trouble.

Rabbi Kuglowski led me to an unoccupied room, where we faced each other on chairs he moved away from a table. Without taking time to introduce the concept of repentance — a concept that had been given such importance by no less than the Jewish sage Maimonides in the middle of the twelfth century — the Patriarch Kuglowski raised his hand and slapped me across my face.

A little boy, unprotected, feeling abandoned. A little boy frightened, like a bleating lamb.

❖ ❖ ❖

I don't remember if I said anything to my parents about what had happened between the rabbi and me, but it's hard for me to imagine I said nothing. I also don't know if the rabbi told them. In either case, what happened in that room never has left me. It might have been a minor event for the rabbi, maybe even for my parents, but it was much more for me. When I think of that moment, I feel once again humiliation, anger, and helplessness. If Rabbi Kuglowski thought his slap would serve some corrective or motivational purpose, he was mistaken. Though I remained in the Academy for several more years without another incident like the one in the basement, my need to escape never diminished. This was so, even after my stellar, award-winning year as a kindergartener.

I received this recognition in a document that my mother had saved and gave to me forty years later, along with other papers, letters, books, photograph albums, and assorted memorabilia. I find humor in the now frayed and discolored paper, and laugh when I look at the signature: *Rabbi B. L. Kuglowski, Superintendent.*

CERTIFICATE OF HONOR
PRESENTED TO
MYLES HOPPER
BY THE TEACHERS AND THE OFFICERS OF
THE RELIGIOUS SCHOOL OF
THE H. F. EPSTEIN HEBREW ACADEMY
FOR REGULAR ATTENDANCE, CORRECT DEPORTMENT
AND DILIGENT STUDY

This Certificate of Honor served as a creative marketing ploy and assured the school of a few more years of tuition. No doubt there were other kindergarten classmates who received one, but I believe I was the only lamb who two or three years later would receive the additional honor of a private meeting in the basement with the Superintendent.

1953. Exodus to a land of milk and honey.

At the end of my fifth grade year, and not a moment too soon, my parents decided we would move to a different neighborhood, and their children would leave the Rabbi H. F. Epstein Hebrew Academy. The timing was right. My older brother would begin high school; my younger brother would have a chance to spend his grade school years not having to climb over a playground fence; I would be relieved of a sadness that had become extreme, and I would end my isolation from neighborhood kids.

When I heard the news, I fantasized I would lead the entire student body in a reenactment of the Exodus from Egypt. In the event, we wouldn't encounter that troublesome Red Sea, but there would be an army of angry parents and rabbis chasing us on chariots.

There was a small problem with my fantasy. Moses witnessed the suffering of his people in bondage. I don't recall my classmates demonstrating anything similar. Even if they had felt oppressed, they would have been as afraid as I had been to just get up and walk out the door. Perhaps something surprising would have happened had I risen from my school desk and said to my people, "Let's flee this place of bondage and suffering. There's a better place not far from here, but we'll have to walk. Who's with me? How about you, Karen?" Joshua could have helped by being my right-hand man, as Aaron was to Moses, but Joshua never would have left R.H.F.E.H.A., not even if he could have played the part of Moses, a part for which he already was more spiritually qualified than I was.

❖ ❖ ❖

Alas, my personal exodus was far more mundane, but still exciting. Our family moved only a couple of miles, but it was to a neighborhood within the same district as the public school I had admired. Our apartment now was only three short blocks from my new school, and soon I would walk to a playground that was even better than the one I had envied, the one that had been so emblematic of much that had been missing in my life. This playground had the same markings of yellow, white, and blue stripes, rectangles, circles, and semi-circles, but its fence was only waist high, and its several gates were never locked. And it was a playground with no rocks.

Karen was still very much in my thoughts as the school year began, so I was surprised by my immediate attraction to a new classmate who differed from her in personality, looks, and style. This girl had long, light brown hair with a little wave that fell over one side of her forehead, and whenever she wore her camel-colored skirt and light beige knee stockings, my attempts at concentration were futile. Because I owned a small pocket knife, it seemed like a good idea to carve her name and mine, with a heart in between, deep into a window frame overlooking the playground. When I was called to the principal's office, I was surprised by how he had been able to identify the love-struck culprit.

"How did you know I did it?"

"There were two clues," Mr. Henderson said. "First, you carved your own name. Second — and this is more than a clue, I suppose — everyone saw you do it."

In spite of his gentle way of speaking to me, I was sure he was angry. But he wasn't, and he didn't slap me. He said that in the future I should respect other people's property. He said, "You should have known that already," and smiled at me. With that smile, I had all the confirmation I ever would need that I was not in exile, and this school was not the lonely diaspora. No, not at all. Indeed, it was a miracle.

2016. A time to gain and a time to lose.

At age seventy-three, my view from the Promised Land encompasses not only what had been gained by my solo exodus but what had been lost, as well.

During the year after I left the R.H.F.E.H.A., I met with Ronnie five or six times, and then we drifted apart. I never saw Karen again or any other of the classmates I had been with since kindergarten. Very often I have asked myself why I lost all contact with my classmates; it has been troubling that no answer ever has felt complete. But several months ago while looking for a misplaced paper, I found a photograph taken in our apartment during my birthday party at age eight or nine. Seven of my classmates are there. Of course, Karen is one of them. We are sitting on a couch and on the floor, and smiling at the camera. Seeing all of us so pleased to be together, I am reminded of something I have known for the past sixty-three years: though it would be a year, two at most, before I would walk away entirely from these earliest of friends, in fact I never had left them behind. I carry them with me even now, as I always have. I miss them, even love them. What I hated was having to be in that school.

It remains as true today as it was then: I knew I had to follow a different path from the one we had been taught was ideal. I was a young boy who yearned for a different sort of Promised Land, and found one with its miraculous playground, far away from the

Rabbi H. F. Epstein Hebrew Academy. But nothing ever has stopped me from wondering what has become of Doreen, Adele, Miriam, Benjie, Jeff, Harold, Ronnie, Joshua. And Karen. Most of all, I hope Karen has had a life that provided her with abundant happiness.

I don't have to wonder, though, what has become of my friend Joshua, the son of a chief orthodox rabbi. I read about him and saw his photograph on the internet. He is, in his own right, a highly respected, orthodox rabbi in Chicago. But, of course he is. In the photograph, he is speaking to a congregation. He has a long, gray beard, and the face I always have remembered as handsome and serious, still is, at least in my eyes. I also imagine that as a rabbi, he is as kind-hearted as he was when we were friends at the Rabbi H. F. Epstein Hebrew Academy.

I should visit Joshua in his synagogue. He is only eighty miles and a lifetime away.

The author & Mr. Henderson, eighth grade graduation

MARGARET KRELL holds an MFA in creative non-fiction from the Solstice MFA program at Pine Manor College. She has taught writing workshops in memoir and essay at various adult educational institutions in the Boston area. Most recently, she developed a course in ekphrastic writing for the Tufts' Osher Program entitled "Objects of Desire." Her essays/memoir pieces have appeared in *The Boston Globe, The Providence Journal,* and *The Washington Post.*

Over the past few years, I have been working on a memoir, Night Stories. *Through a series of interconnected essays and short shorts the memoir tells the story of the entwined relationship between my parents, who were Holocaust survivors, and me. "Tracing my Father's Admonition," included in this anthology, is excerpted and reconfigured from that memoir. One of the frustrations in excerpting a memoir or a novel, I imagine, is knowing that an excerpt can only focus on a facet of the whole work. So why did I choose my father's story? Perhaps because even in* Night Stories, *he occupies the majority of pages. His strong presence permeated our household. My father was charming, generous, reflective, playful. Yet I could never quite trust his gifts, which, out of the blue, could come wrapped in longing and moodiness. I have come to believe a family tragedy is like a glass being broken. My father tried to pick up the pieces. But shards remained. Often hidden from the outside world in the gentility of our well-to-do household, they appeared at the most unexpected moments: A joke that suddenly wasn't funny, a good natured teasing that became too pointed, a distrust for someone deeply devoted. The unpredictable gives birth to the cautious and the insecure.*

So I went to Dresden and subsequently wrote about my father to carve out what was mine. And to finally give the tragedy — the death of my grandparents and uncle, as well as the death of my second cousin, Regina — a place and a name.

BY MARGARET KRELL

Tracing My Father's Admonition

Sara and Israel

When my parents fled Germany in 1938, they were issued German passports, stamped twice with a Swastika and once with a menacing red "J". On the line where the Nazi official wrote the names of my parents, there was an addition reserved for all passports issued to Jews, an extra name, inserted after the first or middle name. The extra name the Nazis gave to all Jewish women was Sara and the name reserved for all Jewish men was Israel.

On the back side of the page with names, my father's passport photograph was tacked down with a round staple, piercing him in the middle of his forehead, a signal that the name from the other side had attached itself to him. Though it was a middle name, it would occupy a place of prominence in my father's psyche: Miami, where my mother and father settled, was hot and humid, a place where a staple could soon turn to rust, and Israel, my father's corrosive middle name, would cause him to fear, again.

The first time I remember witnessing that fear was in 1951 on a Sunday morning. My father had just picked up the newspaper off the front porch. As he made his way back to the living room, his gaze settled on the front page. "You see this?" he said to me, stabbing the photograph of Julius and Ethel Rosenberg with his index finger. As he sank into his easy chair, his hands surrendered onto his lap. "They gave away a secret," he said. Secrets were hidden and dark, but then my father named what for him was more ominous still, "*Und sie waren jüdisch.*" And they *were* Jewish.

Before the Rosenbergs had even been tried, my father had identified them in the past, as if they had already ceased to exist.

Passport of author's father

The Night Story

The night my father told me about the last time he saw his parents and his brother, he also told me not to repeat the story. So I didn't ask the many questions that pushed at my silence, knowing somehow that asking them would touch on a wound so raw, my father might wither away. Before he said good night, he paused at the door to my room. "And one more thing," he said. "Don't tell anyone you are Jewish. It's not safe." I did not know if it was his wish for me or his wish for himself not to tell. But I honored my father. I did not speak his story. I would say I was Jewish only in a whispered voice. So his story became mine; his secret, my own admonition.

In Dresden

About ten years ago, when those two half-bored, half-mischievous cherubs started appearing on ties, bed sheets, coffee mugs, I found myself asking everyone I knew, who painted them. Finally, someone told me the cherubs are part of a much larger painting from Raphael, in which they lean over a coffin. The painting with the cherubs is in Dresden, but that's not why I go.

I have come to Dresden to see the place where my father was born and where he lived until he was thirty-two years old, when he fled in 1938. Shoshana, my father's cousin, has made the hotel reservations and will be coming from Israel tomorrow with one of her daughters and two granddaughters. As I'm dropped off at the hotel, I realize it isn't in the best section of town. The entrance is off to the side, and I have to push a buzzer to be admitted in. The room itself is an efficiency, with a kitchen outfitted in cracked orange Formica. From my father's stories, orange would be the last color I'd expect to see here. Every surface would have been washed in either patina or gold.

I am grateful my hotel room is located in the back of the building away from the street noise, but every half hour or so, a train chugs by. It isn't really that loud, and were I in a happier place, I might not even notice. I might think it pleasant, in a predictable way. But trains have special meaning for those of us touched by the Holocaust, and the impending arrival of the next one preoccupies my mind, makes me anxious. I sleep fitfully, and what comes to me is a memory of a train trip I took with my father when I was very young.

We were traveling from Miami to my grandparents' farm in New Jersey. At about eight o'clock at night, my father told me to wait in the corridor, and when I came back the seats would be magically changed. And in fact, when I reentered the compartment, I saw a bed outstretched in front of me.

"Now how did zat happen?" my father said, teasing me. This was my *Zaubervater*, magic father, the one who could enchant.

Even with his playful speak, I did not sleep well that night, waking up every time the train lurched forward and backward as it stopped at a station, the helmeted lights not shielding me from the glaring bulbs underneath. I slept against my father's chest. He held me so tight, I felt protected but also uncomfortable. Restless. Years later, I would realize my father held me and everyone in my family too tightly, as if he would never see us again.

When I awake in Dresden just four hours later, I reach for a postcard with Raphael's Sistine Madonna, that painting from which the coffee mug cherubs have been extracted. From a distance, the depiction of Madonna and Child is stunning, as stunning as Dresden itself, the Florence of the Elbe, as it was once called. But I cannot get the cherubs out of my mind, not the two transposed onto ties and mugs but the hundreds, whose hair forms the background of clouds. Their faces are in soft focus. And in place of their eyes, there are dark socket pools, as if what they had seen was so frightening they dare not open their eyes again. Or are they even cherubs? Some interpreters say they are unborn children. Such is the imagery that haunts me at Dresden.

The Film

That first morning, I meet Shoshana in the hall, and she tells me she is going sightseeing with her daughter and two granddaughters. After all, I have travelled on my own before. Her friends, Ada and Jürgen, have brought a car down from northern Germany, but there is only room for five and there are seven of us. So while Jürgen chauffeurs and Ada rests, I'm on my own.

Today, I go to the center of Dresden and look for the film that is advertised on sandwich boards all over the city. As I cross an area under construction with several temporary planked walkways, I ask an elderly man for directions.

He points and tells me in German, "Over there." I walk the equivalent of a half a block. Suddenly, the man appears again at my side and points me in the right direction. Then as I'm just about to take the corner to the entrance, he pops up again. "Gerade um die Ecke," he says. Right around the corner. One of those sandwich boards advertising the film stands a few feet in front of us.

"*Haben Sie diesen Film gesehen?*" Did you see the movie, I ask, pointing to the sandwich board with a photograph taken days after the Allied bombing: a robed statue of Goodness, *Das Gute*, stands atop City Hall, her outstretched arm sweeping across the rubble below her feet.

The gentleman answers, "*Ich brauch es nicht zu sehen, Ich hab es überlebt.*" I don't have to see it, I lived through it.

The Facts and Their Heat

Days before the Allied bombing, Raphael's Sistine Madonna with angels at her feet and in the heavens, along with other masterpieces, was taken by truck from Dresden to be stored in a tunnel in Saxon Switzerland, a hilly area outside the city. Dresden was protecting them from the soon to be invading Russians, when the city was firebombed by the Royal and the American Air Forces on February 13-15, 1945. The city caught fire, a fire so hot, it is said to have reached over one thousand degrees; a fire so hot that on a fragment of porcelain, the red Meissen dragon turned green. So much fire that the lack of oxygen created a suction: a mother running with her child tripped, and the baby she carried in her arms was swept up into the wind of the storm. A fire so hot that when bodies were found after the bombing, the heat had sealed their eyelids together. And afterwards, traces still could be seen. Even though the fire had melted the asphalt, footprints remained where people had stood when they died.

I wonder about the kindly gentleman who gave me directions for the film. Is this what he saw, what he lived through?

Cemeteries

Gated and hidden from the street, Dresden's old Jewish cemetery is located behind Pfunds Dairy, a shop listed in the Guinness Book of Records as the most beautiful milk and cheese shop in the world. Busloads of tourists arrive every day to marvel at the hand-painted Villeroy and Boch tiles. In one section, a panel of tiles close to the ceiling shows happy children tackling farm chores, harvesting wheat, milking a cow, and delivering milk in a toy cart pulled by a dog. It is all sweet and a game. Even sweeter are the figures most often associated with the tiles — angels. They find themselves everywhere, especially inside the dizzying scrollwork and behind curved laurel branches, where their privates are discretely covered. Except for the tiles themselves, there seem to be no right angles. Everything is smooth and circular, coming back onto itself. There are no unanswered questions here.

Inside the old Jewish cemetery, the resting place for Jews who died before 1869, it is shady, almost dark, under a canopy of trees. The cemetery is overrun by vines that cling and weave themselves around the weathered stones, which are decorated with traditional symbols. Hands symbolize the deceased was a Cohain (with names such as Cohen, Kahn), a member of the priestly class, who gave the blessing, "May He make His face to shine upon you." Vessels symbolize the deceased was a Levite (with names such as Levy, Levin). The Levites filled the bowl the Cohanim used to wash their hands before prayer. And if the deceased was neither a Cohain or Levite, there were other possibilities for adornment. The grave of Herr *Hirsh*, German for deer, might be adorned with that animal, and the grave of Herr *Löwen*, a lion. Those who had had no distinctive name still found ways to decorate their beloved's grave — with crowns to remind the living that the crown of a good name is worth more than anything else — and even a poem.

> *Here withered is life's once fresh bloom.*
> *You left us too soon.*
> *Your good deeds held such promise.*
> *But death took away all hope for that.*
>
> . . . .

Between some of the tombstones run little iron fences about six inches high, marking off the plots. In most Jewish cemeteries in Germany, these little fences were stolen and melted down, used for the Reich's war effort. In this cemetery, perhaps because it is so hidden, the fences remain.

Jews who died after 1869 are buried in the new Jewish cemetery on the outskirts of town. The tombstones here are less decorated, perhaps just a Star of David. But this cemetery speaks of the Holocaust by what has remained untouched. Some tombstones are half inscribed: *Mein lieber Mann*, my dear husband, and *Unser lieber Vater*, our loving father. These tombstones have a line etched down the middle. And where the inscription for the wife might have been, there is nothing, no name, no symbols, no terms of endearment, nothing but cold, gray granite. The wife was probably taken to a concentration camp and perished there, and so she could never lie next to her beloved husband.

Names in Stone

I knew where to find the graves of Margarethe, Josef, and Werner Krell, my father's parents and his brother. I had read of the place as it was described in a reflection that appeared in a Dresden newspaper, sometime in the 1950s. To prevent it from becoming as fragile as memory, my father kept the reflection protected behind the window of his wallet. It pressed against his hip until the day he died.

But stiff calling cards and phone numbers written on scraps of paper would press against the clipping, flattening it until the folds were so sharp the clipping would tear. Every so often, my father would take it out of his wallet and repair the folds with Scotch tape. But each time he took out the reflection a piece would fall off, and it became smaller, until the writer was left with only a first name.

> *You, wanderer step into our lives and our dying*
> *Following my inner voice, I once again entered*
> *the cemetery of the Jewish Community, which*
> *was destroyed in 1943. In 1946 I saw the*
> *devastated graves, the shattered tombstones.*
> *The traces of this destruction can still be seen*
> *on many tombstones today. [today must have*
> *been in 1950s]*

*[piece missing]. . . at the consecration of the synagogue
which had been built in . . . [piece missing]*

*I remember well all the tormented faces of my
Jewish friends. Over eight years, I was a witness
to the brutal treatment that the Nazi's reserved
for the Jews.*

*I especially remember the cruel "measure against
Jews" at Buchenwald in 1938. All of that is
coming back to me, as I look at the graves, as I
walk through row upon rows of graves. And
then, there it was. The year 1938 was the
prominent number among so many numbers
on tombstones after 1933.*

The date 1938 is prominent in the writer's mind, because on the night of November 9th-10th of that year, the Reich initiated the first large scale violence against Jews. On *Kristallnacht*, Jewish owned shops were smashed and looted, synagogues were set ablaze. Jews were murdered and others were detained in Buchenwald. Though most men who had been arrested were released on the condition that they and their families leave the country, hundreds died in Buchenwald, while others committed suicide in the camp or shortly thereafter. The reflection continues:

*In the back part of the cemetery, a tombstone caused me to pause
and think. Simple, sparse words, and yet powerful in their
accusation, [and] certainty that this is what fascism allowed.*

Krell

Joseph – Margarethe –Werner

*Died together on 22 of May, 62 years old, 60 years old, 30 years old.
The pain of the past, stood – stands – before me again –*

Thousand fold it stands before my eyes. I do not know the life,
the suffering of the Krell family in particular detail. No one,
however, will believe that two generations died of natural
causes in Dresden on the same day.

Brooding, grieving – and full of hate towards the murders,
I left the cemetery. A voice inside me hammered,
Hammered: "Never forget these dead."
                                    Erich [last name missing]

Reflection that author's father kept in his hip pocket

Jewish rights had increasingly been restricted since 1933. Jews were forbidden in museums and other public places, were denied jobs in civil service, and could not teach school. In 1935, they were prohibited from marrying non-Jews and were no longer considered citizens, but subjects. Additionally, the Reich had implemented boycotts of Jewish-owned businesses, subsequently forcing their sale to non-Jews, most often for pennies on the dollar. My grandparents had owned a prosperous chain of shoe stores, where my uncle was employed. By 1938, they must have seen the world closing in on them. In May of that year when they committed suicide, they had nothing.

It is early morning as our group enters the cemetery. We are greeted by the Tolls, the caretakers. They are not Jewish, but Mr. Toll wears a yarmulke out of respect, and Mrs. Toll gives us a bow when she greets us, her shoulders pulled forward in a humble gesture. As I stand in front of my grandparents' and uncle's grave, Mrs. Toll brings me photos she has taken of the marker in other seasons: in spring with pansies, in summer with small begonias, a plant that would not survive the Florida heat, but one my father often longed for, because it was small and cute. And things that are small and cute are innocent and can do no harm. So he believed.

I suddenly remember the angels at Pfund's Dairy, and their cuteness feels overbearing. Even more upsetting is the neat story surrounding the shop, that it survived the 1945 Allied bombing because it was protected by the angels. I should wonder, where were they for the 25,000 Dresdeners who died that day? But at this moment, I can only think about the three forsaken souls beneath my feet.

The marker for my grandparents and uncle is a good five feet across, wide enough for Margarethe, Josef, and Werner to lie side by side. At the time of the tragedy, my father was married to a Gentile woman. Not my mother. The relationship between my grandparents and my father's first wife was strained. So the evening before the tragedy, only my father came to dinner. When my grandparents and uncle said their good-byes, they stood in an upstairs window and waved to my father and did not stop waving.

Gemeinsam Gestorben," Died Together, were my father's words he had engraved on the stone.

I am named Margaret after my grandmother, and my brother's middle name is Joseph after the first name of our grandfather. Joseph was to have been his first name, but when my parents were told that in America only Catholics named their children Joseph, they put that holy name in second place, and gave my brother the name of Ronald, after a friend who fought and died for the Allies.

My grandfather's name was spelled JOSEF. But my father got confused when he arranged to have the gravestone restored in the 1950s, after it had been torn asunder by the Nazis. My father spelled his father's name with a ph, Joseph, like the middle name of his son, my brother.

It would be some fifty years after that error that my brother and

I had the grave restored and had my grandfather's rightful name returned to him.

Sweet Dresden

My father always seemed conflicted about Dresden, reaching towards it, and then pulling back. He had my mother make him *Pflaumknödel*, plum dumplings, once a year, to remember what was sweet, and he kept a picture of Dresden in the hall outside the bedroom he shared with my mother with Goethe's words:

> *You, happy eyes*
> *Whatever have you seen*
> *May let be what was*
> *It was indeed so beautiful*

But it was clear that making peace with what happened was out of reach.

The first time my father tried to return to Dresden, he got as far as the border between West and East Germany. When the Russian guard asked him what he had to declare, my father became frightened, and instead of answering the question, he turned around and took the first flight home. I don't know if it was the question or the uniform that made him run. Perhaps, it was simply the tone and implication. *We don't have to let you in,* which my father, remembering 1938, probably interpreted as *We don't have to let you out.*

The second time he tried to go back, he pleaded with my mother to accompany him. They were on a train going from West to East Berlin. My mother noticed the stop coming up, and suddenly said to my father, "We have to get out here." I don't know if it was because my father was older or if he was daydreaming, which he often did, but he got up too slowly, and was caught between the doors as they were closing. The train took off, dragging him a few feet before it stopped. His hip was crushed. From then on, until the end of his life, my father walked on crutches with a pin in his hip, that same hip that had the reflection pressed against it.

Small Stone

Next to the grave of Margarethe, Josef, and Werner, is the grave of Shoshana's husband, which is marked by a stone about eight feet tall. The monument is flanked by two naturally combed arborvitae, taller than any of us. Only stones set against the outside wall of the cemetery, as this one is, are so impressive in height, and it is unusual in this cemetery to find lush, well-maintained landscaping. I feel Shoshana wants to draw attention to this place, not so much to the large stone for her husband, but to the small marker, only about a foot high set in front of it: *In memory of my mother, Regina Krell, who was detained in Hellerberg and from there was deported to Auschwitz, where she died on March 3, 1942.*

In 1940, Jewish girls in Germany who were sixteen years of age were permitted to apply for visas to attend a farm education program in Palestine. Shoshana was sent there. Her father, my father's uncle, had already passed away, leaving her widowed mother, Regina, in Dresden. In 1942, Regina was detained in Hellerberg, established to house workers for Zeiss-Ikon, which, during the war, made fuses for armaments. Because Hellerberg was located outside Dresden proper, when the last remaining Jews arrived there, Dresden was declared "Jew Free." In Palestine, Shoshana received a few letters from her mother via the Red Cross.

And then she heard nothing.

"You know Margaret, I still hoped, all those years, she was lost and maybe still alive," Shoshanna says to me as we stand facing the gold lettered little plaque. When the truth is too much to bear, we invent what will help us go on. "But then in 1997, when I came here, some-one had the list of those who had been taken to Auschwitz. I saw my mother's name on the list."

The day Regina Krell arrived in Auschwitz, she was killed.

Since the graves of Shoshana's immediate family and mine lie next to each other, I cannot help looking back at the grave of Margarethe, Josef, and Werner. Mrs. Toll comes to stand beside me.

"*Es ist so traurig,*" she says. It's so sad.

Labor Camp

In the afternoon, Shoshana takes her daughter, two granddaughters, and me to find Hellerberg, the site of the labor camp where Shoshana's mother was detained. When we arrive, we see the area is fenced off, not because it is a memorial, but because the electric company houses a tiny substation there. We see men in yellow slickers, because it is raining and cold. We look for traces of what happened here. The area comprises one open block. We walk around the block. It is long and wide, the area inside, as big and as green as a park. Shoshana is determined something must be here. In fact: nothing remains.

I am suddenly reminded of my mother who, when the persecutions in Germany began, was sent to boarding school in Florence. About twenty years after the war, she went back and climbed a hill near the Pitti Palace, looking for her school, and said, "I know it was here." But it was not. We, one and two generations after, do not forget these places that have disappeared, but when we look, they are gone. I wonder, without a marker that tells the story, how long will the memory of what happened here remain? Is this the warning behind "Never Forget?"

Admitting the disappearance, we leave the Hellerberg site and head for the building that housed the former Zeiss-Ikon factory. This is where detainees were forced to labor, walking three miles from Hellerberg to Zeiss and back again every day. The building, now totally revamped, is coldly modern, a box with windows. We walk down dark corridors. At one point we enter a large, empty conference room, space that could have housed factory operations. There is no trace of what took place here, and since this was the place where Shoshana's mother spent her final days, she wants a marker on this building.

In the conference room, we are joined by a representative of the synagogue, Ada and Jürgen, and Gabi, who volunteers at an organization that researches and documents what happened to Dresden's Jewish community after 1933. Someone in our group says we should meet with the proprietors of the architectural firm that we think owns the building. I start to head out with them.

"No, you stay back," Shoshana tells me as well as her daughter and granddaughters. There are a lot of people in our group. Later I learned from Gabi that Shoshanna thought too many people coming unexpectedly and unannounced into the architectural office might intimidate the owner. So I wait in the large empty room with Shoshana's daughter and granddaughters. I wander over to a small window in the corner, perhaps one foot wide by two foot high. It looks out over Dresden, over the dome of the Church of our Lady, the palaces and the bridges that cross the Elbe River. Shoshana's daughter and granddaughters are drawn to this tiny window, too, this slim slit of light, pocket of fresh air. It is a newer replacement window, not the same, I'm sure, as that which was here before. If the previous window opened, would the scent of fresh air have fed the detainees with renewal? And in the evening, when the sky darkened, would the pearl of lights along the Augustin Bridge have given them hope? We watch as the light changes slowly.

Shoshana returns, and she looks miffed. When the group asked if they could put up a plaque, saying what this building had been used for in 1942, the owner of the architectural firm said, *"Wir sind nicht der Inhaber des Gebäudes."* We are not the owner of the building. That stopped the request.

Everyone in the group is quiet. Shoshana tells me in perfect colloquial English, "We got the run around." Now I am miffed, but she seems to have calmed down, *"Na, Ja,"* she says. For a second, that common German expression has taken on a different meaning, No and Yes, a *not no and a not yes*, a place of incompleteness. To remember all the lost names, identify the lost places, takes time, and Shoshana is in her 80s. Will the place her mother labored before she was taken to Auschwitz be commemorated before her daughter passes away? *"Na Ja,"* she says, German for quiet resignation or "That's the way it is."

I wonder, having seen the cemeteries and the disappeared places, if this is really the way it is.

In Memory

Throughout my trip, Shoshana and Gabi have mentioned a plaque on an outside wall of the *Kreuzkirche*, The Church of the Cross, the Lutheran church. This plaque is not mentioned on any tourist brochure of Dresden, nor have I found it even on one website.

It is early morning as I walk the half mile to the church. When I get there, I see no one looking up for a plaque, no one around I can even ask. I go inside. In one room off the vestibule, there is a photographic display of impoverished, indigenous families in a third world country. The room is crowded. The captions are written in German, and though I speak the language rather fluently, I struggle to read it as text. The word order is complex, so I lose my way. I step outside the room to the vestibule, where a woman is selling postcards of the church. I ask her where the plaque is. She vaguely indicates with her hands and says, "*Um die Ecke.*" Around the corner. I go all the way around the church, but can't find it. Back inside, I ask an elderly man, who accompanies me outside. He points up, "*Dort oben.*" Up there. I look up about twenty feet and there it is.

I have a piece of paper with me and copy every word. This I understand, perfectly. I walk back to the hotel and look for the paper to read, but can't find it. I hear the words I want to hear in my head, but I can't find the paper I wrote them on. I walk back to the Kreuzkirche, this time with a writing pad, something with weight, and copy the words, again.

> *In shame and sadness, Christians remember the Jewish citizens of this city. In 1933 there were 4,675 Jews in Dresden; in 1945, there were 70. When their houses of worship burned, and when Jews were deprived of their rights, expelled from their homeland and murdered, we kept silent. We did not recognize them as our brothers and sisters.*

> *We ask for forgiveness*
> *and shalom.*

As I leave, I hear a couple near the church, speaking English. I point to the plaque and say: "Look at that." I translate it for them. They are respectful, but it doesn't move them the way it does me. In all the Holocaust memorials I have visited, I see carefully laid out artifacts. I am moved by how people suffered. I imagine perpetrators pulling a switch, pillaging, pulling a trigger. But I hear nothing from those around me, a reminder of the silence that allowed this to happen. But here, on the wall of this church, are words to break the silence — the people who wrote this plaque realized that silence perpetrates. As Gabi pointed out to me, "*Man bleibt beschmutzt, weil man wegeschaut hat.*" One stays dirty, because one looked away.

That silence devastated me, too. After the war, in the 50s, no one talked about the Holocaust. I remember once in history class, we were studying the Second World War, the battles, the strategies, when someone in the class asked about the Jews and the concentration camps. The teacher said something to the effect that we don't cover that in this class, then he turned his back to us to scratch something on the blackboard. Or perhaps to scratch something out. After all these years, I remember the grating sound of the chalk.

I had come to Dresden, carrying my father's stories, filled with the romance of Dresden, and with the fear. Those first few days, when I was alone, I felt as I had when I was a child — in a foreign land, where nowhere was safe, where I felt unseen and yet exposed.

I have been buoyed, though, by Shoshana, Ada and Jürgen, and Gabi, impassioned advocates for remembering. Their courage has helped me subordinate my trepidation to remember to the consequences of not remembering. I am heartened to see the plaque at the church, the warning against silence, and to learn about yet one more act of conviction. Every year on the anniversary of the bombing of Dresden, thousands of Dresdeners stand firm as they hold hands in a chain around the city to keep out the Neo-Nazis, who have made the date a cause celèbre to downplay the Holocaust, calling the bombing of Dresden, the "German Holocaust." As if this were all.

Stone Unturned

Before he died in 1981, my father became knotted up in guilt and longing and became more moody than he had been before. The shards of what he had experienced always lay unexpectedly beneath his feet, yet he never managed to complete the journey back to Dresden or to reunite with his first cousin Shoshana. In 1938, after the suicides, when the Nazis were looking for my father, for what I do not know, he found refuge in Regina's (Shoshana's mother's) home. After 1938, my father never again saw Shoshana, who had settled in Israel, though he and my mother traveled to relatives as far away as Australia. I wonder if Shoshana was a reminder of his secret: the guilt he felt about not being able to stop the suicides. She was the only surviving relative who had known him during that tragic time. She died in 2011.

Salt

The night my father told me his story, I listened for his steps down the hall to turn to whispers, and then I twisted over on my skinny pillow, thinking about the last thing he said.

"Margaret, Zwergel. This story stays between us." He said both my names, *Zwergel*, munchkin, for I was still a child, and Margaret, for I had heard a story too sad for children.

From that night on, every story I heard became layered with one darker beneath it. I could not hear the Passover question, "Why is this night different from all other nights?" without thinking of the night my father told me his story. A picture always pressed out a picture, a picture with more tears. At the dinner table, even the Morton salt box showed an endless trail of salt. Just as there was always more salt, there was always another girl squeezed smaller than the girl who carried her, until the last girl disappeared into the deep blue box.

AMY WANG MANNING is a writer and editor whose articles and essays have appeared in newspapers, magazines and two anthologies. She is a winner of the Asian American Journalists Association's first-place award in writing. She lives in Portland, Oregon.

This work of creative nonfiction is inspired by an English translation of a Taiwanese household registry that provides a census of my paternal grandfather's household in Keelung, Taiwan, during the 1950s. It is the only genealogical document from my father's family that I possess.

BY AMY WANG MANNING

Extract of Household Registration

The document I have just discovered in my father's abandoned study is labeled "Extract of Household Registration." Though I've never seen such a document before, I know instantly what it is; I've read about these registries, the Taiwanese version of censuses, and a little thrill runs through me. This is the registry for my paternal grandfather's household, at the address where the family spent eight years during the 1950s in Keelung on Taiwan's north coast; there are five pages in English, followed by photocopies of the original pages in Chinese. Suddenly, I have names, birth dates, familial relationships—even, in a few instances, information about education and occupations. It's almost too much to take in all at once.

The registry, maintained by the local police bureau, records twelve family members: my father was living with not only his parents and his three existing siblings but also two uncles, an aunt, and three cousins whose existences were unknown to me until now. My father is described as a high school graduate who left home at age twenty-one to start his compulsory military service. I know one anecdote about him learning Morse code during his two years in uniform, I now know the name of his high school, but I know nothing at all about the years in between. My father is identified as a third son; I always thought he was a second son, but now I realize that he never claimed to be such. He only ever said that he had an elder brother, and so I conjure up a first son who died in infancy or early childhood, so young and so long buried even my mother did not know about him — or whose loss was so painful the family has never been able to speak of him since.

Then I come across something startling. As I cross-reference the entries in the registry, comparing my father's to the others to determine their relationships, I see that my father and his older brother have the same birth date. It can't be. No one has ever hinted at their being twins, and this would be too big a fact to hide, requiring a conspiracy of silence among dozens of relatives and in-laws over decades and continents. It has to be a mistake; perhaps the translation isn't right. Eventually I find out that's exactly the case when I put the registry before a cousin, who deciphers the original Chinese and amends the English version. But I note how readily I was thrown into doubt and confusion, and how painfully slow I was to reach the simplest and most sensible explanation of a transcription error. Knowing so little about my father's past and knowing too much about his anger and defeats means I'm ready to believe anything about him.

Then there's the matter of my father's hometown. Though I've studied the document repeatedly by the time he dies, eleven years after I found it, the name of his hometown, Keelung, never sticks. On the day of his funeral someone remarks that my father is being buried in his birthplace, and I simply nod and go on blindly following my relatives' lead through the unfamiliar rituals and a bewildering swirl of grief and anger, jet lag and adrenalin, guilt and relief. When I finally hear someone identify the town we are in, the name doesn't mean anything to me, except as something I must remember if I hope someday to return to my parents' final resting place. Back home in America I pull out the registry one more time and am genuinely surprised to see Keelung listed as my father's place of birth, the place where he is now buried. I wonder why Keelung has never resonated with me, and then I know: there are no stories attached to it. My father never said to me, "When I was a boy in Keelung," or talked about people or places he knew in Keelung, or reminisced about what he liked or didn't like about Keelung. He simply acted as if it never existed.

So this registry, this laconic document, is all we have for an official family narrative. I cannot accept that. The registry lays out only skeletons; I start to put flesh on the bones, pulling from memories and stories from a long-ago childhood summer in Taiwan.

❖ ❖ ❖

The head of the household, my grandfather, is a man of business. Just look at the registry: "Staff of Tung Hsing Company." He is nothing like his father, a traditional healer whose work filled their home with the pungent scents of medicinal herbs: earth and licorice, astringence and tang. He, a first son, is a full-fledged citizen of the twentieth century, running an import-export business centered on canned fruit. Canned fruit, the food of modernity! He moves his family to Taipei, builds a three-story house on a parcel that will one day escalate in value as the highway and then the subway arrive. But one day there is a dispute with his business partner, and some time later, on another day, he goes his own way, disappointed and a little less wealthy. What of it? He still has enough money to set up one son with his own business, a general store on the first floor of their home, and to send another son across the ocean to study in Mei Guo, the "beautiful country," America. He still has his authority as the head of the household, the patriarch.

Then he begins feeling poorly and goes to the hospital, where the doctors pull aside his family and make grim faces. He is assured everything is fine, but he knows he is being lied to—it is the traditional way, to save the patient from unnecessary distress. He looks out the window of his room and sees a beggar strolling, healthy and happy in the sunshine. He points out the man to his family: I have money and he has none, and he has everything and I have nothing. Take me out of this place. I wish to die at home.

He is taken home and all his family is summoned, including the son who has gone overseas. He lies in bed in a darkened room and waits. One day, two of his younger grandchildren, the six-year-old boy who lives in the house and the six-year-old girl who has flown in with her father and mother from America, creep together into his room; the boy has talked the girl into it, all but dared her. The boy wants to peek at him, to see what a dying man looks like, but then footsteps approach the doorway. Trapped, the children scuttle around the bed, across the room, and into the opposite corner. They hide behind the oxygen tanks, now disconnected and silent. Peeping through the valves, they watch as their aunts and uncles come in, pay homage to the patriarch, weep over him. Later, the girl does not remember how she and the boy got out of the room.

The head of the household is buried on a July day, the heat making his bereaved ones sweat in their traditional rough white tunics. The girl from America whines softly to her mother that her tunic irritates her bare skin. Her mother lectures, scolds, then finally gives in just before the drive to the cemetery and lets her take it off and slip on a light dress underneath: Don't let it show, and don't tell anyone. Up on the mountain where the cemetery lies, the girl skips about with her boy cousin as the adults kneel by the gravesite and burn offerings to the departed patriarch. The gravesite is commensurate with his wealth; it is like a small room, the girl thinks as she takes in the elaborate paving tiles and the ornate foot-high walls. The boy begins a game of tag; as the sun sinks and the mourners chant, the two children run and jump across the graves, their shrieks and laughter echoing off the mountainside. No one says a word to chide them or stop them. Life will go on, as their grandfather well knew.

❖ ❖ ❖

With the head of the household gone, his wife assumes her role as the matriarch. She is from a small coastal town and never went past primary school; the registry lists her occupation as "housekeeping." But she is a first daughter and does not hesitate to make her opinions known. She tells the daughter-in-law who ran away from her, who went all the way to Mei Guo rather than live with her, that her American daughter is too loud and talks too much — girls should be quiet and decorous. The girl is oblivious to how she is perceived; she is too busy keeping up with her boy cousin, who has no compunction in running up to their grandmother and demanding money for a treat. Ever after, when the girl thinks of her grandmother, she sees herself and her cousin holding out their hands. Their grandmother drops a coin in each grubby little palm and the children run off in delight to order bowls from the noodle soup vendor down the street.

The girl goes back to America and the grandmother fades into the recesses of childhood memory. As the girl grows older she understands vaguely that her grandmother is not well; she has something called diabetes and needs medicine that is expensive. Now sometimes when the phone rings, it is her uncle from Taiwan, calling to inform her father about their mother's condition. It seems her uncle doesn't think her father is fulfilling his filial duty. Her father shoots back that he is sending money, and every few years he visits. He comes back from one such trip vastly amused, and tells his now-teenage daughter why: he was doing his laundry by hand and his mother came into the room and began lecturing him on the proper way to wash his underwear. I'm fifty years old, he says, but she's my mother, so she's still telling me what to do. He chuckles indulgently, in a way he never would with his wife.

The girl is grown and living on her own when her grandmother dies. Her mother calls to give her the news. The girl remarks that two nights earlier, she woke up in the middle of the night in a panic, sitting up and crying out no! Her mother pauses. That was the night it happened, she says, you must have felt it. The girl wants to scoff at her mother's superstition. She hasn't seen her grandmother, let alone spoken to her, since that summer in Taiwan all those years ago. But who knows all the ties that bind?

❖ ❖ ❖

The oldest living son of the household is single and his occupation is "nil" when he appears in the registry. It notes that he left home to serve in the military when he was twenty-three. After his two years were up, he must have gone straight back to his father's. He was still there, running a general store and married with children of his own, when his American niece arrived for the summer.

He spent his nights on the second floor with his family, his days on the ground floor watching over his store. Housewares were stacked here, personal items, such as slippers, there. One corner held a row of tall jars with mysterious items inside. His niece did not dare to ask what they were and found out they were candies only after she pointed out a large hole in a lid one morning and her uncle replied, Rats. Front and center was his most prized possession, placed there to draw the eye of every passerby. It was a diminutive refrigerator that held the store's most extravagant items: glass pint bottles of cow's milk. Most of his customers looked at the price and then away. Then his sister-in-law returned from America with her child. Every morning the woman handed him the money for a pint and every morning he went downstairs, retrieved a bottle and brought it back up for his niece. The girl sat at the family dining table and obediently consumed every drop under her mother's watchful eye and his four children's envious stares. How they crowded around to watch her drain the bottle — an entire bottle, every day! Once somebody dared to ask his sister-in-law why she paid so much for this luxury. He would never forget the proud lift of her chin as she replied, My daughter is an American. American children drink milk every day.

He liked the child well enough, and she was fascinated by his store. She begged him to let her work the counter as his children did. He showed her the various Taiwanese coins, explained their denominations. She caught on quickly and soon she was clambering up onto the tall stool, proudly collecting money and making change.

One morning he had just opened the store when a tall white man walked in and pointed at the cigarettes but could not make clear the desired brand. With just enough English to say wait, wait, he hurried upstairs to where the family was eating breakfast. Come, come, he told his niece, and she immediately left her bowl and ran down the stairs after him as he explained what he needed her to do. She went straight to the stool behind the counter and jabbered at the white man, who gawked in response. Flushing with pride, he told the white man, She American, and grinned the way the Americans in movies did, with all their teeth. His niece slid forward a pack of cigarettes, picked up the white man's money, and gave him his change, just as she'd been taught. She said something more to the white man, and he replied, still looking dazed. Then the white man nodded, turned, and left. She ran back upstairs, where the family besieged her with questions until she blushed and hid her face. Oh, to be a little girl who could speak two languages and thus save a sale. Truly, she had done the family proud that day.

❖ ❖ ❖

The youngest son barely appears on the registry. It notes little more than his birth date and order, unsurprising given that he was a month shy of his fifth birthday when the family left their Keelung address. When his brother, sister-in-law, and niece come to Taiwan at the time of his father's illness, the youngest son is engaged to be married; it is a huge blow when his father dies before the wedding date.

They hold the celebration as planned anyway. He is young and in love, and his bride-to-be is a slender, elegant woman, with long ringlets of glossy black hair, who looks like a pinup poised on the back of his motorcycle. He has heard whispers that her face is too long and thin — like a horse's, the more malicious gossips say — but he shrugs them off. It is envy that waggles their tongues. Besides, his nieces and nephews love her, and children are the best judges. That little niece from America in particular has fallen hard, always asking for her and following her around. When he and his bride arrive at the restaurant where they are to celebrate their wedding banquet, the little niece's face falls as she realizes she has been relegated to a side table.

Married, he brings his wife back to the third floor of his father's house. Now the little niece is nearly always underfoot, clamoring to see her new aunt. Bless his wife — she always greets the girl with a smile, bending down to welcome her and give her a treat, listening patiently to her prattling, acting as if every word from her pert little mouth is a joy to hear. When he's alone with his wife at night, he says, You don't have to do that. She won't be here much longer anyway. His wife just smiles again. It's all right, she says. She means no harm. Besides, it can't hurt to be in the good graces of a brother who lives in Mei Guo.

She's right, of course. Years later, they will want to take their own two daughters to the United States, and his brother, now living in splendor on a quarter-acre estate in American suburbia, will sponsor them, fill out a petition for them. Alas, it is not to be. For reasons he will never understand, the petition is denied. The younger brother swallows his bitterness and moves on with his life, though it still rankles him years later when his brother brings the little niece, now an adult, to visit him and he sees the successful American professional she has become, what his daughters could have become. Did his brother really try as hard on his behalf as he claimed he did?

But karma smiles on him. Years later, out of the blue, the niece calls him, seeking assistance. Her father has returned to Taiwan and fallen ill, becoming an invalid; her mother is dead; her mother's relatives are no longer willing to handle her father's affairs. The niece has built her own family in America. She tells him her children are very young, too young for her to leave them. Can he help? He turns her down. He's your father, he tells her. He imagines her flinching thousands of miles away; she will know his rebuke is proper. He's your father, he repeats, your responsibility. She is silent, then thanks him for taking her call and wishes him well. He knows he will not hear from her again.

He hears she is able to finagle his oldest nephew, her cousin, into taking over. Her father continues his decline. With his own health worsening, he pays his brother one visit. He tells him it will be the last, because he does not have the strength to return. By the time he receives the news about his brother's death, he is barely mobile.

He does not attend the funeral, nor does he send his daughters. His nephew will have to represent the family. He hears later that the niece almost did not attend, either; she was scheduled to fly back home two days before, then changed her mind at nearly the last minute. She came that close to missing her own father's funeral. See what happens when a child is raised in America? He thinks of the petition to emigrate that was denied all those years ago—perhaps it was a blessing in disguise after all.

❖ ❖ ❖

The registry remains a skeleton, despite my best efforts to clothe it. Why did my father never mention the registry to me? Why did he have it in the first place? Did he simply abandon it when he fled America following my mother's death, or did he intend to come back for it someday? Did he even remember that he had it?

By the time I find the registry, I have barely spoken to my father for years. His anger has become so increasingly palpable that it is a presence at our family table, a shadow in our family portraits, a specter I need to flee. Without my mother to act as a go-between, conversation is nearly impossible. When he falls ill half a world away, he all but loses his power of speech and starts to sink into dementia. The silence lengthens. He becomes just another name, another half-forgotten ancestor relegated to the archives.

Then he really is gone, and I am out of second chances. The registry is now my solace. Here there are relatives, a family line; here, my father and I are still connected.

Nancy Martin grew up in Kentucky and has lived in Wisconsin over twenty years. She helped her father-in-law write his memoir, *Patton's Lucky Scout*. Nancy was a 2014 cast member of the Milwaukee *Listen to Your Mother* show. She now leads many senior story telling groups and teaches memoir classes. She is in the process of launching a website, Butterfly Drive.

Somehow I haven't written many stories about my father. I very much enjoyed helping my father-in-law with his book. My work on Patton's Lucky Scout *seemed to spark my mom to start writing many of her tales — but Dad passed away a decade before either of those projects began. In my own writings, my grandmother is often featured. When I saw the submission call for this anthology, I immediately thought of my daddy's letter home to his mother (my beloved Mama Brown) during WWII. My dad was one of those "salt of the earth" guys. While Dad generally seemed easy-going, he was a man of strong principles. I hope you enjoy my story and that you, too, come to know my dad.*

BY NANCY MARTIN

The Teetotaler

My first understanding about alcohol came one summer day in the early 1960s when we had visitors. Daddy was not at all political, but, a master electrician, he held an office in his local 369 of the International Brotherhood of Electrical Workers (IBEW). The IBEW is associated with the powerful and even more political American Federation of Labor & Congress of Industrial Organizations (AFL-CIO). When some big-wig national officials came to Kentucky for an important meeting, Daddy was asked to host them. Plans were made for the two gentlemen from out of state to have dinner at our house before he took the men to that evening's official function.

We entertained all guests in our big lower-level family room, cooled by the only air-conditioning in our house. The floor was usually strewn with our cars, puzzles, and books, but we had stuffed everything in our big toy closet. We knew it was a special occasion since Daddy put on a tie and it wasn't even Sunday. When the men arrived, everything started out fine. Still in grade school, I accepted my role of smiling and being polite to the company. I had told them where the bathroom was in case they needed to go. Mom had dinner almost but not quite ready. Dad came downstairs asking, "Can I get you fellas something to drink while you wait?"

Simple enough question, or so it seemed.

"I'll take a bourbon on the rocks," the tall one answered.

"Just a beer for me," said the other man. "Whatever kind you have will be fine."

Daddy rarely seemed at a loss for words, but this time he stopped cold in his tracks — even reeled back on his heels a bit as his mouth dropped open. I could tell something was wrong. You could almost see gears turning as he tried to figure out what to say next as a good host.

"Well...Um...My wife makes the best sweet-tea in town, and we have some lemonade if you would like that. We keep milk and Kool-Aid in the fridge for the kids but, other than water, that's all we have to drink in this house."

The tall guy got a funny stunned look on his face. One eyebrow seemed to rise up, and he puckered his lips. He was the first to recover. He said, "I think I'll try that sweet-tea. I keep hearing that is the thing to drink in the south."

The other guy, with slicked down Brylcreem hair, was trying to back-pedal out of his request. "Sorry brother, I didn't realize this was a dry county."

"This is not a dry county." Daddy's tone turned stern. "But this is a dry house." It was the same tone he used when I hadn't done my chores. I knew by his voice and the look on his face, Daddy did not approve of bourbon or beer — at all.

Only a handful of states have dry counties now, but during the 1960s, probably half of Kentucky's 120 counties still prohibited the sale of alcohol — despite the fact that the state was, and still is, a major producer of bourbon. And while you theoretically weren't supposed to have alcohol in a dry county, back when I was young, package stores often sat along the road just over the county line. The package stores had a big plastic sign featuring a beer brand on top and the store name added below. Some showed neon beer signs in their windows or hard liquor posters. As we drove to visit my grandmother every weekend, I noticed their parking lots sure stayed full of cars with Mercer County license plates — dry county people making frequent stops at a nearby wet county store.

The other absolute I knew about alcohol was that bourbon stinks when they make it. There was a distillery on the country lane leading to my grade school, and when vats of sour mash fermented, it stank to high heaven — worse than fresh skunk road-kill. As we drove past the distillery, we made sure all car windows were rolled up and even closed all vents to keep out any yucky air. When the wind blew down the holler, the smell nauseated me so much that I didn't even want to go outside at recess time.

In the passage of time, I learned other bits and pieces of information related to alcohol. Sometime in the late 1960s, Daddy made his momma, my beloved Mama Brown, give up her membership in the Women's Christian Temperance Union (WCTU) — a group determined to rid the world of demon drink. The group's famous pledge read: *I hereby solemnly promise, God helping me, to abstain from all distilled, fermented and malt liquors, including wine, beer and hard cider, and to employ all proper means to discourage the use of and traffic in the same.*

Daddy agreed with WCTU philosophy, but every time Mama Brown attended a local chapter meeting or read their national newsletter, he said the stories sent her blood pressure dangerously high.

In Kentucky history class we heard about Carry Nation — a fervent champion of the temperance cause who would take a hatchet to wooden barrels of whiskey in saloons. In fact, Carry Nation was born in Garrard, a dry county even today, which is the next county east from Mama Brown's Mercer County.

During high school, I also started learning about Europe, particularly England and France. My father served in the Army during World War II and spent several months in both countries. Daddy told me that he had never ever, in his entire life, drunk any alcohol — not one drop. It seemed to me that England had a whole lot of pubs that sold ale. I also developed an impression of France that everybody drank wine, even kids. In all the Saturday afternoon war movies about World War II, soldiers seemed to drink a lot of "spirits" — putting the two together, I did start to wonder. How did Daddy manage to serve in the Army, especially in Europe, without drinking alcohol?

Over the years, I never heard of any particular reason why Daddy stayed so vehement against booze. He had his own personal code of conduct that he stuck to — he never drank, never smoked, never lied, never gambled, and he never ever broke his word. He had a moral compass that never wavered from his true north. You knew that if Daddy gave you his word on something, you could believe him and count on him.

While Daddy didn't officially gamble, we did occasionally watch harness racing at the Red Mile in Lexington. A pretty good judge of horseflesh, he'd eye over the contenders and, just as the bell sounded, announce his pick. "You know that number seven horse looks mighty sound tonight," he might say after betting closed. Sure enough, the number seven horse would win that race, pulling away easily from all other contenders. Daddy didn't pick for every race, but he was always right when he did.

I don't know if memories of that horrid sour-mash distillery smell of my youth or the influence of Mama Brown and Daddy put me off alcohol. Truth be told I do occasionally have an amaretto or a margarita, but I've never been much of a drinker. At my wedding in 1989, our caterer diplomatically handled my staunch teetotaler Baptist relatives and our enthusiastic bourbon-drinking friends, commenting that she had to restock the bourbon supply for our reception twice — a first in her long history. The need to restock twice seems even more remarkable to me in light of how many tee-totalers were there. When our limo left for the airport, the Baptists were still visiting in the quieter side room and our friends still danc-ing away the day on the parquet wood floor. My parents financed most of my wedding expenses, but my husband and I covered the open bar bill.

My father passed away in 1997, and Momma died in 2010. When we were cleaning out their bedroom closet, I found a box of over two hundred letters, yellowed with age. Daddy wrote them to his mom during World War II. They were a treasure to find and read. I saw the younger version of the man I knew, scrawled across those pages. Then I came upon a letter written from California, just before his discharge.

The letter read in part that he had a fight with his hut-mates on Saturday night. The other guys he shared his tar-paper hut with had been playing poker and drinking. Somehow they had decided that night, that my dad, PFC Brown, should have a drink before he got out of the Army, and they tried to force it down his throat. Dad's anger was still steaming in the letter as he related how he fought them off. By golly, he meant it when said No. Alcohol spilt all over their quarters and clothes, but none down his throat. Daddy reported that the ringleader apologized the next day for their actions, after he sobered up. Family rumblings said Daddy scrappily fought all comers as a teenager, but around me, he always seemed calm, rarely even perturbed. This letter is my only glimpse of the fighting side of him.

I can't say I ever really questioned Daddy's veracity that he never drank alcohol or gambled, but that letter banished any shadow of a doubt. Whenever I am badgered about not going along with the crowd, I think of Dad's letter, and it stiffens my resolve. Here's to you, Dad!

PATRICIA ANN MCNAIR'S short story collection *The Temple of Air* was named Chicago Writers Association's Book of the Year, Southern Illinois University's Devil's Kitchen Readers Award, and Society of Midland Authors Finalist Award. McNair's fiction and creative nonfiction have appeared in *American Fiction: Best Unpublished Short Stories by Emerging Writers*, *Prime Number*, *River Teeth*, *Fourth Genre*, *Brevity*, *Creative Nonfiction*, and other publications. McNair is a book reviewer for *Washington Independent Review of Books*, and she teaches in the Department of Creative Writing at Columbia College Chicago. Visit her website at patriciaannmcnair.com.

When my mother died in 2002, I got possession of boxes and boxes of her family documents. "Climbing the Crooked Trails" is fueled by that cache of letters, articles, papers, and photos. There is nearly a century's worth of these things, but this piece focuses mainly on what I discovered among those from the early 1900s when my grandfather, Victor Hugo Wachs, was a motorcycle missionary for more than a decade in Korea. My mother was born there in 1924, the fourth child of her family.

My grandfather's letters are dated from 1910 to 1926, and the photographs packed away with them have set me on a meandering path, wandering and wondering. My husband, the visual artist Philip Hartigan, and I have mounted print, sound, and text installations based on this material in Chicago and in California, but I continue to consider and explore these papers in a variety of forms. There is no particular order or no reason to these crooked trails I follow, and yet, here I go. Again and again.

BY PATRICIA ANN MCNAIR

Climbing the Crooked Trails

A (grand)daughter's thoughts on a motorcycle missionary, Korea, mothers, fathers, grandparents, faith, love, loss, doubt, invention, creation, things kept, rambling, grief, home, writing, and places I've never been.

"...climbing the crooked trails..." my grandfather, Victor Hugo Wachs, wrote about his experience on the back of a motorcycle in Korea in the beginning of the last century, the place he had been assigned to carry out mission work by The Korea Quarter-Centennial Movement of the Methodist Episcopal Church. I found this line among his letters, the ones from the boxes in my mother's apartment.

Sylvia (my mother) died in 2002 after what was both a long and much too short illness. We knew it was coming for more than a year, so we had time to plan, to talk, to get things sorted. Still, after her death, the task of going through her things (the things of a seventy-eight-year life) was overwhelming. Not just what to keep, what to share, what to discard—but the discovery of all there was. And, more specifically, all there was *left*.

Boxes of letters and photos and negatives and documents and bits and pieces that my grandmother passed on to my mother. Decades of correspondence from my mother to hers, and decades of correspondence from her parents, from my grandfather mostly, to people I knew and didn't, and to and from more places I'd never been. Things written before and after the birth of my mother.

My mother was a writer; she told me that I needed to write, too. She gave me assignments, small writing prompts, when I was a little girl and while she worked at her editor's job. In summer and on school's-out days, I would write stories for her. This collection of writing is like another assignment left to me by my mother.

❖

My mother was born in Korea. I've always loved telling people that. It's a cocktail party line, a thing I say to make myself sound like I have an interesting past, something to tell. Something more interesting than the truth: despite a short list of places I've called home, I've lived ninety-eight percent of my life in the Midwest. In fact, today I live less than a mile from the hospital (closed now, fallen into disrepair) where I was born.

But. My mother was born in Korea. When I tell people that, there's often a hiccup in the conversation, a squinting of eyes over the high-ball glasses by my fellow cocktailers.

"Are you Korean?" someone usually, invariably, disbelievingly will ask.

Look at me. I'm a mutt, like most Americans. A bit of that, a bit of this. A smidgen of French. Ancestors from England, Scotland, Germany, Ireland. My hair shines reddish in the sun. I freckle. I am not Korean.

When I was little, I thought I *was* Korean. I thought that being born someplace meant that you were of that place, you could name yourself when you named the place, and, consequently, you could name your children that, too. Your grandchildren. How many of us are called American, despite our origins, our ethnicity, our lineage?

"You're not Korean," my mother told me once when she heard me say to a playmate that I was.

"You are," I said.

"No I'm not."

"But you were born there." How old was I then? Whom did I tell? It might have been Julie Peterson, the little blond girl who was adopted and lived next door. The girl who was prettier than me, who had her own room while I still had to share mine with my brother. What did I have that she might not?

"I was born there," my mother said, nodding, ironing. She had a day job, but I remember her standing in our kitchen, ironing. "Still, I'm not Korean. And neither are you."

We are not Korean. I am not Korean.

❖

Chicago, Illinois. Bath Spa, England. Mount Carroll, Illinois. Cedar Rapids, Iowa. Interlochen, Michigan. San Miguel, Honduras. Niles, Illinois. Mount Vernon, Iowa. Prague, Czech Republic. Johnson, Vermont. Solon, Iowa. Florence, Italy.

These are the places I have lived. Some for years, some for weeks: a month at least. Places I've called home.

8855 Greenwood Avenue. My first address. 299-3165. My first phone number. A series, each, of digits set to memory so that I could use them to find my way, if need be, to the place I grew up. The first place I'd ever really been.

I've been thinking about the idea of place — I often do — and the idea of being in a place. Of being placed. Not just my situation, where I am situated, but also that other sense of place. As in the abstract, emotional way of place. Like: "Let me tell you where I am at with this." And the logical, debatable, pro and con of place: "This is my position." "Here's where I stand." To me, these ways of considering place (physical, philosophical) are inextricably bound together. Despite my having been a travel writer (like my mother) and having over the years taught in four different countries, there are many, many places I have never been. Among these is Korea. And yet, from reading my grandfather's letters, I have visited this Korea of my mother's origin, of my grandparents' and aunts' and uncle's lives in the early 1900s. This is not a place that exists any longer, not exactly as it was then, and yet I visit it, again and again.

❖

Author's grandfather and grandmother on a Harley Davidson in Korea

My grandfather, so the family lore goes, was the first person to ride a motorcycle in Korea. That's a version of our history I believed for years. Decades. Here's a modification of it: my grandfather was the first non-Asian to ride a motorcycle in Korea. That may be closer to the truth, a truth I might be able to find if I did the research. Internet. Books. Records of motorbike sales. Etc.

I have to admit, though, I'm not really interested in the truth. Not in this case. I am much more interested in the lore, the mythology of such a claim. A white man (Victor Hugo Wachs) named after a poet on the seat of a motorcycle traveling over the hills and rutted roads of early 1900s Korea, a bible in his rucksack, a baby on his back, and my grandmother wrapped in her skirts and settled in the sidecar.

Does it matter if he was the first rider there, the second? The twentieth? The story, to my mind, is spectacular, incredible enough without any more heightening.

❖

My grandparents were missionaries. I was never baptized.

❖

My father died when I was fifteen years old. He was an atheist. His parents, like my mother's parents, were Methodist. Evangelical.

My father was an atheist and I was never baptized, and my mother, who was born in Korea to missionary parents, had her own doubts and split with the church in her twenties.

So when my father died when I was fifteen, when he was fifty-five, I thought, though I didn't know, that if there was a god, a heaven and hell, my father would be going to hell. Despite his having reared and loved a family, despite his having worked on causes, social issues, despite his propensity for occasionally taking in strays — people without family or direction — to live in our home (good, Christian work, all of this), my father, the atheist would go to hell.

❖

I've been thinking about the word CHOSEN. It's all over my grandfather's letters, and I suppose I am a bit embarrassed to admit that until recently, I hadn't known that it meant KOREA.

It's an interesting word. Full of meaning and possibility. To choose. To be chosen.

Chosen. I wonder if all those times my grandfather wrote that word at the top or the bottom of a letter (addressee, signator) he even noticed the American word behind it.

Chosen. Selected.

Did he feel chosen to be in Chosen? Or did he choose this place to be?

Chosen. To have a calling. To be called. To be chosen. To be in Chosen.

❖

Among my grandfather's letters is one from my great uncle, my grandfather's brother Paul. I remember Paul slightly. To me when I was little, Uncle Paul looked just like my grandfather, only slighter, shorter, perhaps. Or maybe taller. Thinner. I have a shimmery image of him standing near a car in a church parking lot, smiling in the sun even though it is — of this I am sure — a funeral day; whose, I don't recall. Grandmother's? The memory is not fully there, like some of the photos I've found, bright and shadowed in a way that makes me not certain what I see. I remember liking Paul immensely, finding him funny and kind and warm in a way that was genuine to my child way of knowing things.

In his letters to my grandfather in Korea, Paul speaks openly and with great concern regarding his doubts about faith, about God, about his own calling.

These letters from Paul are among my favorites among the hundreds. The uncertainty attracts me. The things he does not know. The things he may or may not believe. His place in a world he does not fully understand, may not trust, cannot be sure it is as it appears.

This is a place I know. The place between doubt and commitment, between knowledge and faith, between stay and go.

Paul became a minister despite his doubts. Or maybe because of them.

❖

I want to say something more about when my father died.

I remember that some days after his death I was sitting in a car in the parking lot of a Kmart, waiting for my brother or my mother to return from running an errand. It was autumn, cool, and dark in the evening. My father died in October.

An Asian girl approached the car. She had pamphlets in her hand. She was a Moonie. A follower of Reverend Sun Myung Moon. A Korean missionary of a sort herself, I suppose.

My window was open, and so she stopped, looked in. Teenager to teenager. She didn't speak much English, but she said something about God, about Reverend Moon, about heaven, maybe.

I had been struggling with the idea of my father, my good father, going to hell. And so I asked her, implored her to tell me I was wrong, to explain it to me if I was right, why, how. To make me feel better about things.

The more I spoke, the less it seemed she wanted to hear. Perhaps it was because she didn't understand my language, or perhaps it was because she didn't understand my pain. She looked frightened, I remember now, scared of whatever it was I wanted.

And what did I want? Kindness, maybe. Comfort, certainly. Reassurance, yes.

The girl backed away from the car window and said, "Call this number." She pointed at a pamphlet, one like she had given me, one I didn't recall taking but found in my hand. "Call this number," she repeated. And even as she said this, it sounded to my ear like she was speaking from memory like you sometimes do when you learn a new language. Answering by rote.

I carried the pamphlet with me until I didn't anymore. I never called the number.

❖

My mother and I, in the last years of her life, talked about assimilation. It was after that particular September 11th, and there was fear everywhere, a distrust of "the other."

She surprised me by saying that she thought people of different cultures should try to fit in to the culture they inhabit. Assimilate. My left-leaning mother with very few prejudices thought we should all try to blend in. In practice, I know this desire, to look like you belong, to not be the obvious interloper. Though I am a regular tourist, a frequent visitor to places other than my Midwestern home, I am not eager to call attention to myself for this and the various ways I am different from the locals.

Sometimes I can pull this off. The many summers I taught in Prague, for instance, I walked the narrow city streets with purpose, planning my routes ahead of time as much as possible, pretending

I knew where I was and where I was headed even if neither of these things was true. And I wore a Czech scowl. There is a certain dourness to Czechs — at least in Prague, but I've seen it in smaller towns, too — that middle-aged residents wear on their public faces. More than once I was asked directions, tram information, questions I couldn't understand, much less answer. And not just by tourists, but by locals as well.

I had assimilated.

But consider this: my grandfather in trousers and shirtsleeves and cap, goggles over his eyes, astride his Harley or his Indian (depending on the year), motoring into a tiny Korean village. My grandmother in flowing Victorian skirts, petticoats underneath. Her fine brown hair pulled up under a wide straw bonnet. Their four children, blond and grey-eyed and easily burned by the sun. Playing Ring Around the Roses and London Bridge Is Falling Down.

Could they be more "other" than their parishioners, their Korean hosts? Could they be any less assimilated?

❖

I am surprised and a little dismayed by the lack of information about my grandfather's children in his letters. My mother was born in Korea in 1924. Her older sister Marie Evangeline was also born there. Her brother Miller, too. El Rita, the oldest child, a girl, was born in the United States and carried to Korea in 1910.

Wasn't there something to say about these little American children among the Koreans (and Japanese, soldiers mostly) in this tiny Korean town?

"The baby has been sick," in one of the letters.

Which baby, I wonder.

❖

My mother told me about a time when she came back home to Vermont where her family had moved after her parents' sixteen years of mission work. This was years after they'd arrived back in the states, sometime after she'd left home for college, for jobs. She'd been working in Arizona in a Japanese relocation camp. Keeping records for the government, hoping, in this time of world war in 1943, that her work with the Japanese might be meaningful, helpful — in the way so many people wanted to be useful then. Her infancy connected her to Asia and Asians, but she didn't know at the time, or didn't want to believe perhaps, how wrong the Americans were in this relocation, this internment process. How vengeful were their motives. How racist.

My mother lost her virginity in the Arizona desert. She delighted in telling me this story when I was old enough to hear it. Under a desert moon and with a handsome man — maybe more boy — in his early twenties, and a bottle of wine. A rattlesnake interrupted them.

And even though she was a woman in the desert, when my mother returned home from thousands of miles away, a long and slow journey by train across our vast country, my mother was still a girl. A teenager.

Her parents didn't meet her at the station. They were off somewhere, church business. There was always church business, my mother told me. And so she, home after months in the desert, had to get herself to her house (was it the same house she'd left? Her parents moved when called, parish to parish). She had to wait alone (her older siblings already grown, married and gone) until her parents returned from their business.

When my mother told me this, I was appalled. Didn't they want to see her? Hadn't they missed her? Weren't they worried?

"It didn't matter," my mother said.

We were driving in Vermont when she told me that story, fifty years after her return from the desert. She was showing me the towns where she'd grown up, the house where she'd lived. Places, until then, I had never been.

She looked out the car's window at the river she told me they used to cross on foot when it froze in the winter, a shortcut to school. She told me how her principal, a family man, would go out first after the freeze, testing the ice. Making sure it was safe for the children.

❖

Among the letters and papers is an order form to Montgomery Ward, a hand-written shopping list of items to be sent from Chicago, just a few miles from where I sit now as I write this, to Korea. "Auto hat" in navy. Bathing suit. All sorts of stockings in various sizes, materials, and colors. A "low bust" something or other, I can't read the word there, but squeezed on the same line: "figure" and "corset." "Home games," quantity one, price fifty cents. Tennis slippers and tennis balls. And rubber sheeting for a dollar-twenty-nine. The practicalities of their Korean life. Goods. Garments and games.

❖

An excerpt from a letter my grandfather's aunt sent to Korea: "Tony got killed Wednesday week before last. The little fellow had gone out to the hayfield with your father. He had been working so hard to dig out a groundhog and became so hot and tired that he lay down in the shade of the wagon on which they were loading hay to haul it in. The wagon ran over him and he died next morning. We put him in a nice little box and buried him in the shade of the twin maples north of the garden. And none of us felt ashamed of the tears we shed for poor little faithful Tony. It just seems so lonely. He was after your father all the time like a little boy. I wish we could get a nice fox terrier. It doesn't seem right without a dog."

And at its end: "Please write more often and let us know if something is wrong."

What must it have been like to await word for weeks, sometimes months, from someone on the other side of the world? To read of accomplishments and loss from folded sheets of handwritten notes, struggling to make out the words among the pen marks? And here are my grandfather's letters, typewritten mostly, carbon copies on something like tissue paper, wrinkled and disintegrating at the edges, other words and letters showing through from the flipside, a way to conserve paper, to use everything since they were so far away from everything, shops and supplies and conveniences.

A short note among those from Korea. This one to New York. The National Cloak and Suit Company. A note that must have accompanied a pair of shoes, style number something or other, size something, chosen from a catalogue. "Please send one size larger," my grandfather requests. How many weeks did he have to wait for a new pair of shoes?

❖

My grandfather was an inventor. I remember this from when I was a girl and he and my grandmother lived in Wapakoneta, Ohio (the hometown, by the way, of Neil Armstrong, the first man to walk on the moon, another place I have never been). My grandmother by then was a double amputee, diabetes, I think, and her days were divided between bed and wheelchair. My grandfather rigged up a complicated pulley system to help him get her from one spot to the other. She'd sit high in her bed and hold on to this thing that looked like a trapeze, her upper body still strong. My grandfather would hoist her onto the rig then, and lift her some, and together they would get her into the chair.

There is a photo among these Korean ones of my grandfather's motorcycle with some huge thing in the sidecar. A machine, big as a boy. It's a cook stove, I discover from his letters. Something he's made to carry on his journeys, fueled by wood, a way to have hot meals on the road.

A small thing I remember among my grandfather's inventions: an empty thread spool with a nail hammered in it and bent parallel to the spool's curved surface. He used this as a toothpaste roller, threading the emptying tube between nail and spool, and winding it flat to get every bit of toothpaste out of it.

I know these things he made are available now, versions of them, and conveniently so. Toothpaste rollers, hospital pulley systems, portable cook stoves. Invented by others, not my grandfather, others who profited from their innovation and industry. But I wonder, was anyone more satisfied by a hot meal cooked on his portable stove than my grandfather would have been after hours riding the crooked trails over Korean hills and rivers in the early 1900s? Or more satisfied — no, delighted — than I was as a little girl, as I watched the white worm of Pepsodent issue from its tube while I wound it tighter and tighter around the spool of my grandfather's invention?

❖

In the last year of my mother's life, months before I would go through her things, before I would find these letters and files and photos, we brought hospice into her home. They did what they do to get started, visited and asked questions and made a plan and told us the rules. No medical intervention, they said. Something for the pain, for comfort, but nothing to prolong things. It seemed both reasonable and not: no IV if she got dehydrated? Nothing for her body's deep, unquenchable thirst?

And they asked if she wanted a chaplain to call?

"No," she said emphatically. I was surprised.

We sat in her living room, Mom in her soft, nubbed reclining chair, me on the blue velvet couch, the hospice worker on a wooden dining chair with her back to the view from the balcony, through the tall, tall trees that grew up from the courtyard below. It was July and early in the afternoon, the sun wouldn't set for hours.

When my father died in my fifteenth year, I struggled with heaven, with hell, and I told my mother about the Moonie girl I'd met, I told her about my fears.

"Is that what you really think?" She asked me back then when I said I knew my father was going to hell because he was an atheist, an unrepentant sinner. Hell despite his kindnesses, despite his social conscience. And she said something like, "Oh, Darlin'." She looked sad. "I don't think that's what will happen."

She didn't say any more, and I didn't ask; it hurt enough for us to get this far in the conversation, we both cried so easily. But I always thought that she had another idea about heaven, about hell. About God. I always believed that she believed, even though she no longer practiced any religion (an interesting word for this: practice, never a master, forever in training).

So, just a few short months after the hospice social worker had come to survey us, to make a plan, my mother was close to the end. We all knew. She knew. The phone rang.

"Yeth," she said into the receiver. She didn't have her teeth in, they hurt her now, her mouth was raw and dry all the time.

"Yeth," she said again. I heard the creep of annoyance in the edge of the word; a telemarketer, I thought, someone invading our little time left.

"Who told you to call?" she said. And she twisted at the buttons of her robe, an anxious fidget that I've inherited: twisting. tapping, fluttering. "I thaid I don't want to thpeak with you."

Who is it? I mouthed when she looked at me, but she waved away the question.

"How dare you call me when I thaid I don't want to thpeak with you." She pulled the phone away from her ear and looked at the keypad, searching for the disconnect button, pushing a number first, or the pound key; the touchtone sang loudly through the receiver.

"Damnit," she said, and found the right button. "It wath that chaplain," she said. "From the hothpith. I hung up on him." And I could see that she was angry, her fingers tapping and twisting on her lap. With no real handset and phone cradle to slam it into, hanging up on the man brought her little relief.

❖

I go through these boxes of letters and photos over and over again, looking for what I don't yet know, what I might have missed. I am looking for my mother and for her father, my grandfather, for who I am because of them. I am looking for my place here among these letters, the photos, the stories and memories they conjure. I am looking for my father, too — fathers and daughters — I understand now, even though he isn't in these boxes. I don't think of myself as one of those sorts of people who ponders the big questions, but I can't deny that I am looking for the big answers.

❖

My mother believed in sentences. She believed in words, in stories. When she was a little girl, nine years old, she had an assignment to write about her best friend. The family was back in the states by then, but hadn't fully settled, had already moved once or twice. My mother didn't have a best friend. Often the new kid, always a PK (preacher's kid), many years younger than her closest sibling. I imagine she was lonely often, "the other" still. She was a toddler in the Orient, and a girl in a small town in a vast country where people spoke the language she knew, but had memories she didn't. So she read books. Lots of them, and always. A pastime her father and mother encouraged (she told me about how the family read *Les Miserables* by Victor Hugo out loud together in the evenings) and a pastime she loved.

My mother's best-friend essay was about her bookcase. It was made of bamboo and carried across the world on a ship from Korea, placed in her room and filled with books, the first iteration of her serious habit of keeping. The bookcase held what made her happiest, was home to her closest friends. How many times did she tell me this story, the one about her own story, and about a teacher who read it and loved it, who encouraged her to keep writing?

We visited that teacher on our trip to Vermont. The woman must have been in her nineties, but she knew my mother still. She had the dozens of travel books and geography texts that my mother had written and sent her copies of once they were published. They shared memories, these two, mother and teacher, while we sat in what the teacher called the parlor — a slightly formal room with doilies on the arms of chairs and a smell like dust and liniment.

"I still remember your story about your bookcase," my mother's teacher said and my mother nodded and smiled.

Have I said yet that the bookcase, my mother's best friend, is my bookcase now? Have I said yet that it has moved around the Midwest with me, sat in my bedrooms, my living rooms, my kitchens, and now in my bright and airy sunroom where I sit to write in my journal?

"Over the Backbone of Korea" is the name of an article my grandfather sent to *Motorcycling and Bicycling Magazine.* Among his letters I find one to the editors of the magazine, a thank you for their having published another article he'd sent them and a cover letter to this one, this "Backbone" one that was (used to be) "enclosed herein." And it is here, in this eager and hopeful letter to an editor that I find my place, next to my grandfather. Not my grandfather the missionary, not my grandfather the motorcyclist, not even my grandfather the father. My grandfather the writer. The one who tells stories and writes them down, who holds the stories out to others with slightly shaking hands: read this, will you? Please? And if by some chance you do, and you like it, find it interesting, perhaps you will share it with others.

And here, too, in this place of writers, my grandfather, me, is my mother between us. A travel writer with hundreds of articles and dozens of books to her credit. A woman who was drawn to travel to places she'd never been since she was a baby in Korea, a toddler in Japan, a child in Vermont. And drawn, too, to write it down.

Here we are, my mother, my grandfather, me, going places. Here we are, side by side, climbing the crooked trails.

CAROLOU NELSEN grew up in Oak Park, Illinois, and graduated from Northwestern University and later the University of Wisconsin–Milwaukee. She lived her adult life in the Milwaukee area and has been a school social worker and an artist. Her newfound interest in the written word was inspired by a writing class held in her retirement home. Her two adult children have given her four grandchildren and a new great grandbaby.

The possessions and records of my brother Bob's World War II service time are few, but I cherish what I have. Recently I have been working on family scrapbooks of pictures and mementos to hand down to my two adult children as their history.

I rediscovered a letter on my computer written by Bob when he was stationed on Guam as Commander of a B-29 crew. Their mission was to bomb Tokyo, Japan, and its surrounding war factories. At first, I was not yet ready to read his words. When I finally did, my first thought was, "This is pretty well written." And then the memories of our lives together as we grew up came flooding back.

Bob was seven years older than I, so of course I always looked up to him. When he went off to war and I was in high school, we were finally coming together in understanding, and the age difference seemed to lessen, but this new layer to our relationship was not to continue. So I take comfort in this writing of memories seventy years later.

BY BOB FRITSCHEL & CAROLOU FRITSCHEL NELSEN

I Had a Brother

I had a big brother. Seven years my senior. The family story goes that when Mama pushed my wicker baby carriage to Bobby's school yard, the teacher said that he had told her two years earlier that he was going to have a little sister. When we were kids, he often reached his foot under the dinner table to give me a teasing kick. The table was scratched but I never felt rejected.

> *This is how I spend my time here on this god forsaken island of jungle and a crushed coral & Macadam airstrip. I sleep until 10:00 or 10:30 AM when the heat makes me get up. I do little detailed stuff and eat from 12 to 2.*

Bob was a B-29 pilot in the World War II Pacific Theater. I felt lucky. So proud! His letters came at random, written on light-weight pale blue Air Mail paper. No one was supposed to know the whereabouts of any World War II troop stations. But before embarking overseas, he gave his family a date code to use in his first letter home from "somewhere in the Mariana Islands." Each letter brings back memories of our pre-war family life.

> *The whole lazy atmosphere changes about 24 hours before a mission. Odd eating schedules, meetings and briefings come one after another.*

We check and double check every piece of equipment. The ground crew goes over the ship with a fine tooth comb. Long wagons rumble up and ugly, heavy bombs drop into their appointed places. Then, strangely, everything becomes quiet. In the fast rays of the sun, the flight crews take to their ships. The ground crew chief and his men stand to one side, their jobs done, and their faces intent.

Our parents said that I walked late. Little feet pushing a Kiddie Car at age one and a half years was easier. But when Bobby returned home from a hospital tonsillectomy, I upped and chased him gleefully 'round and 'round the dining room table.

The flying crew takes over. Last minute instructions and inspections. Each man checks his station and equipment for the last time. Pilot and co-pilot coordinate. Navigator and radioman are wedged into position ready for vigilance and listening, which might well mean the difference between life and death for 11 men out there in the darkness. Each gunner is checking his turret. Everyone is ready now. Tense. Quiet.

Waiting. I had to wait when the chickenpox came to our house and a yellow quarantine card was hung on the front door by the health department. I was warned not to enter my brother's room or I might get "Bobby's Spots." What were those spots and why was he in bed all day? I did sneak in and later found myself in my bed, decorated just the same.

Engineer start engines! After silence, a metallic whine and a roar, all four props are turning. In the glare of a landing light, the crew chief grins, makes a circle with his thumb and forefinger and waves the ship out. The air is filled with an unholy roar now. Slowly moving ahead... checking, always checking. Watch the RPM. Brakes off and she rolls faster and faster. Won't you ever lift? Easy on the flaps. Airspeed OK. Wheels up. Everyone relaxes. The co-pilot lights 2 cigarettes and hands one to the pilot.

Bob loved flying. Perhaps inspired by the Lindberg flight when he was a child. He earned a pilot's license at age twenty and took each family member up for a short ride in a Piper Cub. The passenger seat was in front of the pilot in that very small cabin. Taking off was a thrill for me. "Look out that right window, Carol," he said. When I did, he promptly tilted the little plane onto its right wing!

It settles back into routine now. The hours of waiting. Nothing but inky blackness and the knowledge that you are a part of a powerful armada out to drop death and destruction on an enemy who asked for it. A gunner cracks a joke. Not very funny but everyone laughs anyway.

Laughing. A hearty unrestrained laugh. Tilting away from the dining table on the back legs of his chair (much to our mother's objections) to laugh at a joke.

You wish you could sleep — you're tired — but you can't. The engineer sits like a statue watching his gauges. Everything in order now. A can of tomato juice is passed around.

Dinner is over. Who would wash the dishes and who would dry? Take turns? "Mom! She doesn't get them clean." Snapping the towel on my legs. Sometimes chasing me out into the back yard 'round and 'round the apple tree.

Navigator to pilot: We're an hour out [of target]. OK 'Let's put on the monkey suits, boys'. The heavy, cumbersome flak suits go on plus the helmets. You'd think it was Easter Sunday the way everyone takes such care.

Can I have the car next Saturday night, Dad? So handsome dressed up for a high school dance! Pssst. Is my breath OK, Sis?

There's the coast [of Japan]. I see a glow at 12 o'clock. OK. Keep your eyes open. Fighter at 3 o'clock. Don't think he sees us yet. Yes, he's coming in. Skid her! Skid. Funny. That flak suit doesn't seem a bit heavy now. OK. He's lost us, I think. That was close. I think he hit the left wing but I'll be damned if I'll get out and look. OK. Hold your fire unless he opens up again.

The bombardier is checking his switches and sight for the last time. Flak at 12 o'clock. Flak at 2 o'clock. Flak at 10 o'clock. On altitude!!

Oh, oh. Here comes a searchlight. They've got us. Blinding light. Flak be hanged. We're on the run. Bomb doors open. Look at that flak cloud. We'll have to go right through it. Sounds like rain on a tin roof.

Bombs away! Pack her up. Let's get out of here, H. P. (Hot Pilot nickname). Good job. Fighter coming in at 7 o'clock high. Blackness. Good. The light left us.

Learned about motors in the garage with Dad by taking apart a Model T Ford purchased with high school job earnings. I suggested the half-and-half paint job. Traditional black on one side and red on the other. A hit at Oak Park High School and the kid sister was pretty proud.

Well. That's that. A good job. The guys are chattering but I wish I could sleep. Awake with a start. It's light and bumpy. There has to be weather just to make it interesting on our return trip. More long hours. On and on. Pilot from navigator: There's some music on the radio compass so we'll be in in an hour. Who is that? Glenn Miller? Yeah. In The Groove. There's the sun again. Heading in.

Tuneful whistles coming up the street after the early Thursday morning delivery of the Oak Leaves local paper. Music. Lots of music. Taught himself to play the French horn because the high school band had enough trumpets. Walked around the house annoying us by tooting just the mouthpiece. How did he do all that homework with the radio playing in his room? And still made National Honor Society.

There's the field. Prepare for landing. I've got about enough gas to hit the end of the runway. Easy. Easy. That does it. Down!

Along the embankment ground crew is sweating her in. Broad grins now, vainly trying to see if she picked up any holes. Can't see much as she flashes by. That's OK boys. A couple of patches and check #4 [engine] and she'll be as good as new.

Let's see. It has been 30 hours since we have seen a bed. The sack will feel awfully good. I feel like I've been through a wringer. There's the Chaplain checking us off with a big smile. Yeah. We made it. What'd you expect?

Other letters ended with the characteristic "Don't worry. We'll get this war over and come home." But at seventeen, I became an only child. Our little family changed forever.

Bob was stationed on Guam from March 1945 to April 14, 1945. The "Battlin' Boomerang" B-29 was downed in Tokyo harbor on its fifth bombing mission. My brother was declared missing in action in May 1945 and buried at Punchbowl Memorial Cemetery at Oahu, Hawaii, in 1948.

Jan. 26, 1921 - April 14, 1945.
He was 24 years old.
70 years later, I still remember.

Bob Fritschel

JOANNE NELSON'S writing appears in *Midwestern Gothic, Redivider, Brevity, Consequence,* and other publications. She is a contributor to *Lake Effect* on 89.7 WUWM, the local NPR affiliate, and gives presentations on topics related to spirituality and writing, the personal essay, and creativity. Nelson lives in Hartland, Wisconsin, where she develops and leads community writing programs, maintains a psychotherapy practice, and, of course, adjuncts.

Learn more about Nelson at wakeupthewriterwithin.com.

"In My Office" grew out of a prompt to write about things that seem dissimilar. Looking around my office, I noticed the picture I describe in the essay. My study of the photo revealed more and more about me, my brothers, and our family, the closer I looked. Soon everything about the picture became important — those cups, the curtains, that ivy in a planter hung on a wall. Everything in the photo dates us and explains us, even the family's economic and cultural status. As the drafts piled up, I was sent to the internet time and again for answers. What were those cups called? Are they the same ones we got with green stamps at the grocery store? One thing led to another, and my research trips resulted not only in the answers to my questions, but days and days of internet advertising pop-ups as a continuing blast from the past!

BY JOANNE NELSON

In My Office

In my basement office I keep a framed picture of my brothers and me, circa 1967. The three of us stand behind a kitchen table that features a three-tiered birthday cake and Currier & Ives coffee cups centered on matching saucers — enough to indicate the presence of our grandparents. The coffee looks freshly poured, an equal amount in each cup and no lipstick smudges on the rims. Burnt-orange colored Melmac creamer and sugar bowls wait, forks are at the ready, and an ashtray rests left of center. A black planter with gold filigree hangs on the far wall, and an ivy's forever-green leaves loop in tangles above Steven's head, the vines trailing down behind his back. The boys wear plaid shirts, buttoned high, although Bill's shirt is only half-tucked into his corduroys — a detail I'm surprised my father, with his sharp words and critical eye, let slide. I'm dressed in a white turtleneck. The collar is rolled down to prevent that choky feeling, and there's a shadow between the shirt and my neck that emphasizes my pale skin and long features. The sight of my close-cropped pixie cut, hideous in the days of long, folk singer hair, makes me want to reach into the photo, grab the little girl's hand, and run away with her.

Bill holds a fishing pole, the new reel silhouetted against the pastel wall. He looks happy. Clearly this is his scene: the lit candles on the cake in the foreground are way too many for me. Steven, looking grim, is positioned a shoulder behind Bill. I'm tucked in between them, one hand in Bill's and the other unseen behind a chair. Steven drapes his arm across me. My size suggests I'm about five, which would make Bill fourteen and Steven twelve. We stand close together and take our cues from those on the other side of the table, the adults waiting for just one decent shot without all that goofing around so they can eat before the coffee gets cold or the candles burn the house down.

Despite its being Bill's day, I try to claim the moment. My jaw juts forward and my contorted grin shows all my teeth. My eyes are crinkled shut as I lean towards the camera. I'm an irritant to the adults, and if I don't knock it off soon I'll end up crying in my bedroom. Only Bill's smile appears true and emanates beyond his face, through his tall body, and into the gift he holds. He'll soon be able to move on — even the simple present of rod and reel a ticket to somewhere else. Steven's eyes are distant, his mouth a tight frown. His expression reflects either some parental cruelty tossed his way or bad shutter timing; he's already closing his mouth for the final S of "cheese," while Bill and I continue enjoying that long E. A metaphor really: Steven was so often out of sync with the rest of us.

In my office I also have a white board hanging above my desk. It's covered with computer logins, phone numbers, and papers stuck fast with magnets. Things I shouldn't forget. One scrap sports the heading "Dual Perspective" and a partial definition, "the distanced narrative persona." The note has escaped my monthly purging of outdated to-do lists and inspirational quotes for over a year, earning its keep again today by sending me back to that photograph, back to wondering about Steven's arm draped over my shoulder.

Protection, I decide, continuing to want the story to be about me — not about a random positioning while Steven waited for the song to be sung and cake to be served. This occurs to me only after staring at the image so long I begin to feel the brown ridges of the vinyl chair against my thumb and hear the cupboard door open as my mother reaches for milk glasses. Maybe he sought comfort in the feel of my thin shoulder, connection with the one person not likely to yell at him. Me as stabilizing factor — forever the baby and a girl to boot, always a blessing after two boys. A foil between our parents and him, that third side of the triangle to shift the focus elsewhere. Me as shield, the relatives telling my father: you can't be hitting a girl like you do those boys.

I don't want to be the baby, though; the photo spells this out. I'm pulling away, while Steven tries to hold on. The weight of his arm is heavy on me. As we grow I'll join the chorus of voices wanting him to work more, drink less. Our age difference no longer important, our heights nearly the same, I'll encourage all manner of change, using every technique I learned in my social work classes. But he'll remain the same sad boy in the picture, and I'll forget, for a long time anyway, how much solace is given just by standing next to someone. Then, years down the road, protection no longer possible, I'll give a final gift of comfort when I hold Steven as he takes his loud, terrible last breaths, his long face skeletal, his belly swollen from a broken, alcoholic liver.

The shelves next to the office door are jammed with vertically and horizontally stacked books interspersed with mementos: snapshots of my daughters, a crystal jar of paperclips, unlit candles, more framed pictures. All evidence of who I am now. One photograph includes my father, his mother, my brothers, Bill's three kids, and me. I stand next to Steven and he rests his arm on our nephew's shoulders, his mouth in that same childhood oval, as if he again missed the signal to smile. Steven had yet to meet his third wife. I hadn't had children.

Those bookshelves hold the answer to why I'm down here: the manuscripts recounting stories of escape or return and the mementos that tell their own suspended, yet scripted tales. It's the dual perspective of the little girl held close by her brothers in a corner of the kitchen, safe behind glowing candles, and of the woman at her desk in a basement office — the soft hum of the dryer in the background, pictures of her family surrounding her — who just wants to tell about it.

ANNILEE NEWTON teaches high school English in Houston, Texas. She is the creator of Cupboard Sundries, a blog about food and life.

I have grown up with the family myth of the Kentucky land. My family of English immigrants forged its new identity in Kentucky, and I've always suspected that I could find pieces of my identity there, too. I knew I would end up in Kentucky one day, rooting around and trying to piece together a past. But I always thought that Grandpa Leet would still be around when I was doing this. Writing "Leet" was an attempt to try to bridge the gulf that has always existed between Grandpa Leet and me. I wanted to understand where I come from, and I wanted to understand Leet.

I used text from my Great-Aunt Clara's 74-page genealogical record to help me research and construct Leet. She donated a copy (excerpt below) to the Campbellsville Public Library in Kentucky.

...Leet met a cheerleader, Joyce Martin, after he transferred to Taylor County High School. They were married in 1951, just before Leet was to ship out to Korea. President Harry Truman had declared a police-action and sent the National Guards from around the U.S.A. to Korea to stop the North Koreans. As is would happen, they were stopped at the 38th parallel.

As Chief of Firing Battery, Leet was attached to the 623rd Field Artillery of the National Guard. The 623rd was heavily involved in the Battles of Heart Break Ridge and Punch Bowl. General Ridgeway, the General who replaced General Douglas MacArthur of the Far East Command, presented Leet with an Accommodation Medal for those battles.

Leet worked four years for the American Louisiana Gas Company and retired as District Superintendent of the Florida Gas Transmillion Co. In 1991, he married his high school sweetheart, Mildred Slinker, after her husband, Gus Robertson, had been dead for ten years.

BY ANNILEE NEWTON

Leet

There are places in the world, like Provence or Thailand, that do not require justification to visit. But when you tell people you're going to Kentucky for a few weeks, you must explain yourself. Sometimes this works, "I have family there." And that might be the end of it, the mystery of your motivation solved.

Sometimes, though, the listener's face just grows more perplexed. "But why are you *going* to Kentucky?" Then I say, "I am going to prune my dead grandfather's pear trees that he planted twenty years ago." I'm not sure why this explanation goes down easier. Perhaps it's the specificity. Or perhaps it's because inexplicable behavior is expected when dead people are involved.

When I observe the pear trees, I realize that I am vastly underprepared to prune these trees. These pear trees are at least one story higher than Grandpa Leet's barn. Thanks to a farming book, I understand how pear trees usually work. Pear trees are grafted together from a rootstock and a scion. The rootstock is planted in the ground, and the scion part of the tree blossoms and fruits. The rootstock gives strength and foundation, while the scion is chosen for the taste of the fruit.

There is a wound where the two are joined.

I stalk around the trunks of the five pear trees, looking for the wounds. I can't find any. It's possible that I don't have enough knowledge to be able to observe the wound, but it's also possible that these pear trees aren't grafted. I wonder if Grandpa Leet grew these trees from seed. I wonder if Grandpa Leet ever pruned these trees, these epic, sprawling, gargantuan trees. I think about how all of the fruit falls to ground, uneaten and turned back into earth.

And I don't prune my dead grandfather's twenty-year-old pear trees.

❖ ❖ ❖

When I was five years old, I followed Grandpa Leet into his vegetable garden. I had important stuff to talk to Grandpa about. Mrs. Casteel, my kindergarten teacher, had asked me what I wanted to be when I grew up, and I told her that I wanted to be a farmer. So I brought a book up from Mississippi for Grandpa Leet to read to me, a farmer book about horses with lots of pictures.

So I waited until Grandpa Leet started walking through his garden, sifting through his vegetables. He was behind a tall border of tightly planted corn, and all I could see were flashes of his hands moving up and down the stalks. I wound my way through the maze and ambushed him.

"Grandpa! Will you read this book to me?"

His plaid shirt was unbuttoned; he balanced a Camel, unfiltered, between his lips. He set the box of corn on the ground and looked at the book. "Now, Annie, I don't know anything about horses."

"But you're a farmer," I said. Plus, it was a book. Worse come to worst, we could learn about horses together.

"I'm a different kind of farmer," he said. And he turned away and started picking tomatoes. I walked back to the house.

❖ ❖ ❖

In my memory, Grandpa Leet is always holding or sucking on a Camel. He kept a package of cigarettes in the front pocket of his plaid shirt. Over the years, doctors would present Grandpa with all kinds of horrific eventualities as a consequence of his smoking. Stop, they would say, over and over again. If you don't stop, you will get cancer, you will have another stroke. Over my dead body, Grandpa would say. A couple of decades later, Grandpa Leet's second wife's grandson, Gus, Jr., would tuck a package of Camels into a different shirt pocket just before they lowered Grandpa Leet's corpse into his grave.

❖ ❖ ❖

I stand at the place where tamed land has turned wild. The place where Grandpa Leet used to plant his corn and tomatoes. This place is way back, on the part of remaining Newton land that is farthest from the edge where the road diminishes into dirt. I know this land has secrets, and I know Grandpa Leet had the benefit of learning these secrets first hand from his father, Samuel, who learned it from his father, John Henry, who learned it from his father, John Thomas. But whatever know-how needed to turn the land back into food has died with Grandpa Leet. Dad has a nugget or two of growing wisdom, but I think he gathered that on his own. I only know enough to be able to pick up on the echoes of the culture of my family once preserved. I only know enough to realize that I know nothing. I know enough to understand that I've lost something, something important.

I used to close my eyes and try to remember Campbellsville, but the only patch of dirt that materialized in my mind was this place that used to be Grandpa's tomato garden.

❖ ❖ ❖

I didn't go to Grandpa Leet's funeral. I was in London when I heard about Grandpa Leet's death, in a pub called The Dove on the banks of the Thames. The Dove has been around since the early 1700s, back before all those first migratory Newtons crossed over the Atlantic and started farming. Grandpa Leet's sister, Great-Aunt Clara, developed a taste for digging through the flotsam and jetsam of the past to uncover our story. She said that once you start to view and review the records of the people of the past, it becomes addictive. She reconstructed our story from gravestones and pieces of paper, and this story begins with

Thomas Newton, a man who died before 1772. Thomas is the beginning of Great-Aunt Clara's family tree, the beginning of the whole Kentucky farming tomatoes thing, and he's the beginning of me. Well, he's a beginning. According to Great-Aunt Clara, connecting the unknown with what you know helps you to understand the past. And understanding the past helps you to understand the present.

❖ ❖ ❖

I'm in Kentucky, and Grandy is showing me around Campbellsville.

"Now, Leet's Momma and Daddy built that house." She points to a small brick house with a front porch. Just a regular-looking house. It rushes past the windows of the car, and I look back at it, knowing I'll never be able to distinguish it from all the rest of the regular-looking houses. Grandy watches me. "It's good to know something about where you come from," she says.

Grandy and Grandpa Leet were childhood sweethearts over at Campbellsville Elementary School. During Grandy's second year of high school, Grandy's family moved across the state to Murray, Kentucky. "Now, that's a traumatic thing to happen to a person at that age," Grandy says. She and Grandpa Leet were separated. Grandy married a gospel singer farmer and built her life in Murray. Meanwhile, Grandpa Leet graduated from Campbellsville High School and married Grandma Joyce. Then he immediately went off to fight in the Korean War with the rest of the boys from town. Grandpa Leet was a sniper. When he blew out his eardrums, Grandpa could have gone home with a Purple Heart, but he refused. He didn't want to leave the rest of his battalion. At the end of his service, the army offered Grandpa Leet a full scholarship to West Point. Grandpa Leet refused. He wanted to go back to Campbellsville, return to his wife, and be a farmer. So he came back and started taming his father's land, turning the wilderness back into food.

"You'll be wanting to go to that graveyard," Grandy says. "There's some Newtons buried in that graveyard. They've had plots, bought and paid for, for hundreds of years. Leet and I lived over in that neighborhood by the university, and we would walk through this cemetery most days to get to school, if it wasn't too muddy."

"But, Grandpa Leet isn't buried there?"

"No, it's the funniest thing. You know, he was sick for a while there at the end, and I'd ask where he'd like to buried, and whether he'd like to be buried in Campbellsville with his family. He'd never answer me. Finally, very near the end, your daddy was up there, and he said, 'Now, Dad, you've got to tell me where you want to be buried,' and Leet finally told him that he wanted to be buried in Murray. So he was."

"Did he ever say why he didn't want to be buried back here?"

"No, he didn't. Maybe he didn't have very good memories from here."

"Maybe not," I say.

❖ ❖ ❖

I observe a dead leaf. It is gently decomposing. The spine of the leaf is still there. The straight forks and the network of veins are almost all still there, too, but the in-between areas have disintegrated away. Only the structure of the leaf remains, and it casts a lacy and delicate shadow.

I realize that I have no idea what all of the parts of a leaf are called and that I have to borrow words from human anatomy to think about them. I don't know what to call the in-between parts that aren't there anymore. The connective tissue? The skin?

❖ ❖ ❖

I'm talking to Dad on the phone and walking around the land. I wander into Grandpa's outdoor kitchen. There is an old avocado refrigerator, a sink, and a brick fireplace. Rust is eating into everything, and everything is cobwebbed and lacquered with many layers of the dirt and moss and dust that coat outside things over time. Roots from a nearby pine tree have broken up the foundation.

"What I'm saying is, I think we can save the fireplace, Dad. It's still standing strong."

"Good. That's where Grandpa used to do all his canning. He invented a lever with an arm to go over the fire. He cooked over the fire in his cast-iron pot, just like in the old-timey days."

"I see the lever. It's still working." I crank it up and down a few times with my free hand. "That's a pretty smart contraption, Dad."

"Of course it's smart. He was the smartest person I ever knew. Except for me, that is."

"That's a great line, Dad. Maybe I'll save it and use it about you one day."

◆ ◆ ◆

On my last night in Kentucky, I have dinner with Cousin David and his wife, Debi. David is the son of Grandpa Leet's youngest brother, Charles. "Leet was like a father to me," says Debi. "You know, Annie, your grandpa taught me the right way to can our vegetables.

"All my life, I would lose some cans of tomato juice. Some cans would go bad and some wouldn't. The old folks around here say that if your cans get spoiled, it's because a woman went around the vegetable garden when she was on her monthly. Annie, I can't tell you how many times I got fussed at by my daddy because the canning got spoiled. After me and David got married, I noticed that Leet's canning always turned out fine. One day I asked him about it. I asked him if it was my fault our canning always got spoiled because of my monthly. Leet laughed in my face. He said, 'Debi, you don't believe that old wives' tale, do you? Let me show you what you're doing wrong.' And he did. And when the next canning time came around, I only lost one jar of tomato juice."

"What were you doing wrong?"

"Well, your Grandpa Leet juiced his tomatoes, just like we did, and boiled them on the stove, just like we did. You boil it until the foam goes away. What Leet did different, was he added the sugar and salt before he boiled the juice. I added the sugar and salt individually to each of the jars. And that's where the corruption was getting in. He also told me the very best tomato juice mixture was one-half Early Girls and one-half Better Boys."

"Did you tell your family about this? Did they start canning the right way?"

"I told them all about it. But they wouldn't change their ways."

❖ ❖ ❖

I remember Grandpa Leet in his outdoor kitchen. Moving around behind the screen walls, early, early, when the mist was still coming off the corn fields. Grandpa Leet making coffee. That smell of coffee and morning mist stays with a person through the decades. Grandpa Leet making scrambled eggs with sausage. Grandpa Leet making country ham and grits with red-eye gravy. Grandpa Leet cooking ground sausage over the open fire in a monstrous cast iron pot, removing the sausage from the heat, and cooking flour in the remaining grease until it turned the color of oak. Adding milk little by little to make gravy. I remember eating this gravy over biscuits and sliced tomatoes from Grandpa Leet's garden. Maybe Grandpa Leet used Better Boy or Early Girl tomatoes, but I don't know. I can make this gravy, but I don't have a garden with Better Boy and Early Girl tomatoes. I will learn how to grow a garden that can feed me.

❖ ❖ ❖

I bring more farming books up to Kentucky this time around. The thirty-year-old me throws a blanket in the grass under a tree and starts to read them, one by one. My favorite book is about permaculture. Permaculture is a method of farming that attempts to establish a different type of agriculture, a permanent type of agriculture. My permaculture book tells me to watch and observe the land before I plant anything. In the best of all worlds, the books says, a farmer would observe her land for an entire year before she planted anything. She would spend that year noticing things. She would notice the place where the water pooled in the spring, and she would plant watercress there. She would watch the sunny spot by the forest turn shady as the trees became lush in early summer, and she wouldn't plant eggplant there. She would ask old Mr. Leon at the end of the road which variety of okra does the best around these parts, and then she would propagate that type. She would find the patch of earth between Grandpa's old outdoor kitchen and the five pears trees he planted, the spot where the wind brings the coolness of creek to freshen the air in even the hottest days of summer, and she would plant mint there. She would notice that the July fireflies come out every evening around 7:00 and start to disappear again around 8:30. She might even notice an errant firefly in her bedroom one evening, flashing into the nonresponsive black void of her bedroom. She might run around the bedroom in her pajamas until she has the firefly cupped in her hands, and then she might release it back outside where it would fly away into a flurry of other communicating lights. Observation is how a farmer learns about the potential of her surroundings. It's how she learns about the land.

PAM PARKER is a New England native who calls suburban Milwaukee, Wisconsin, home. Her work has appeared in numerous print and online publications and has been featured on WUWM, a Wisconsin Public Radio Affiliate. She co-edited the anthology, *Done Darkness*, about surviving depression. She tries to chip away at the stigma of mental illness by being open about her personal struggles. She has received awards from the Wisconsin Broadcasting Association, the Wisconsin Writers Association and the Wisconsin Academy of Arts, Sciences & Letters. Learn more about Pam and her work at pamwrites.net.

This story begged to be written. It pleaded, poked, and haunted me until I could sit and breathe life into it. The information which my biological uncle discovered about my grandmother — including her letters from a notorious mental institution — were an incredible find for anyone, a stroke of luck to an author and a tragic "what if" to me personally.

In facing the contents of "The Blue Cardboard Box," I had to confront not only all the horrible things my grandmother had experienced, but also some of my own demons. To be honest, though it was a gut-wrenching process, I have to own up to some pride. I am proud to have found the courage to write this story and share it. I like to believe my efforts would be appreciated by my grandmother, Velma Gasteyer, and the boys she gave up for adoption, my father, James D. Parker, and his brother, Richard Schnell.

The Blue Cardboard Box

A blue cardboard box arrived on my doorstep. I had asked for it. The mailing label bore my mother's penmanship but the box contained another woman's story, the stuff of nightmares. Even so, I had asked for it.

The woman's name was Velma Gasteyer. She was my biological grandmother. I knew we shared the obvious — my father, her son. When I'd opened an email from my mother and clicked on an image of Velma as a young woman, my breathing had stopped. We also shared eyebrows, nose, a square chin. At that moment, I knew I had to request the damn box.

It had been offered to me when my sister and my dad's brother, both sleuthing for information about family biology and history, found each other. Uncle Richard, Dad's brother, had collected the information in the box. I learned snippets of Velma's story through phone calls and emails.

"She had a lousy life."

"She ended up in a nuthouse."

"There's a box of her letters. You should read them. You have to write about her."

I declined offers of the box, until I saw that picture. But now, I couldn't bear the thought of diving into it. The box seemed cursed.

Velma and Dad had been dead for years. Uncle Richard, the finder, died. His daughter died. His grandson died. The deaths were piling up.

I clutched a grey prayer shawl and rocked, the blue box nearby on the coffee table. Golden maple leaves swirled outside the bay window. Autumn and death and this sad, awful story. I didn't know what I would find in the box; I only knew jumbling questions and feelings.

Would Dad want me to open it?

Probably, I murmured to the dust motes in the sunbeam.

Would Uncle Richard insist I lift the cover?

Definitely. Finding Velma, or at least her story, had been a mission for him and my sister. How many families had similar stories that had been lost, forever?

I could no longer ignore this gift, even while it felt like a curse.

I stalled a few weeks, moving the box to the ping-pong table in the basement, but the burden or summons demanded action. Finally one day, I lifted the sturdy lid and faced a six-inch thick pile of Xeroxed papers. Thumbing the stack, I resisted reading the summary typed report on top. I jumped to the end of the summary to see my uncle's sign off. He wrote of finding and visiting her grave and typed, all caps, in blue ink: "SHE WAS MY MOTHER," which was followed by "End of search.... Amen."

I skimmed the pile, which was mostly letters from Velma. The return address was always the same:

Velma Gasteyer
Pilgrim State Hospital
W. Brentwood, L.I., N.Y.

Her greetings repeated and echoed, a refrain of reaching: Dear Daddy and Abbie; Dear Gram, Aunt M and Mildred. The closings were often the same, too: All my love and kisses, Velma. Followed by lots of x's.

The pages were reminders of life before email, when handwritten letters were the means to share thoughts and feelings. I thought of friends and old correspondence — Libby, a penpal from Cardiff, Wales. Dead too young from lupus. In high school I'd exchanged notes with Nancy, a brilliant, funny friend. Dead too young from breast cancer. I sat down on the dingy throw rug, legs crossed like in kindergarten but without childish innocence.

Deaths, memories of friends, and letters pressed on my head and shoulders. I tried to focus on Velma's letters, but her pretty penmanship distracted me. Lovely swirling penmanship from another time. From the days when cursive writing was an art form.

Dad had fine penmanship, too. I closed my eyes to see his swirling signature, James D. Parker.

❖ ❖ ❖

I returned the pile of letters to the box and read Uncle Richard's summary.

Velma's placement first at Bellevue Hospital and then at Pilgrim State followed a visit to her grandmother in New Jersey in early 1947, when Velma was twenty-nine. During the visit, she had a "spell." In his notes, my uncle elaborated: "She became impossible to cope with, she became violent in her behavior and soon required professional help. This led to placement in Bellvue Hospital (sic) for a short time."

What factors led to the spell, which her father later referred to as a nervous breakdown? Why at Velma's grandmother's house?

I didn't have a lot of information. What I had, all I had, was in the blue cardboard box.

Velma's mother died in childbirth when Velma was fourteen. Her family lived in New Jersey. After her mother's death, her father moved Velma and her brother to Massachusetts.

Good grief, I thought. Her mother died, a baby sister or brother died, and her father moved the family several states away? Probably for a job. It was 1932, Great Depression time, people moved anywhere for work. Velma lost close contact with her grandmother, aunt, cousins, and friends.

Not good grief, just grief. Maybe Velma's father — my great-grand-father — needed to move several states away to cope, work, and move on himself.

Grief.

❖ ❖ ❖

I begin to understand my compulsion to open the box. I know a few things about the power of grief, grief unacknowledged, grief unconfronted, grief buried. I don't want to go there again.

Shortly before her commitment, Velma worked as a nurse's aide in Washington, D.C. She was almost thirty years old, employed, and unmarried, though she was engaged twice according to the summary. First, "for some time" to a man named Richard Gazverde, who had returned from the war "a different person." Before her hospitalization, she was engaged to a man named Eddie Towle. He is never mentioned again in the summary.

She had given up two sons for adoption. I'll never know if this was her choice, or if her father demanded it (as could be expected in those times). Her first baby, my father, was born on February 6th, 1937, when Velma was nineteen. She named him Jon. The second baby, born the next year, on May 14th, 1938, I would later know briefly as Uncle Richard. Both boys were probably delivered in Springfield, Massachusetts, but my uncle's birth certificate was never discovered. My father's birth certificate does not name his father. Were they half-brothers? I want to believe her sons were created in love, but given Velma's youth, they could easily have been created in the throes of hormones and grief. I know what I did with my grief after Dad died. I'm lucky not to have landed with unwanted pregnancies.

She grieved the baby; I grieve the man she never knew.

❖ ❖ ❖

I try to follow the threads in the summary. Velma's mother had died in January, 1932, fifteen years before Velma's visit to her grandmother "early in 1947." Maybe the visit happened in January? Maybe she was thinking of her mother's death?

My siblings and I used to mark my father's death day, which to this day we call "Dead Dad Day," by excessive drinking. For me, that meant drinking to the point of ridiculous singing along to the juke-box at the Red Basket, the town bar, which happened to be across the street from the cemetery where Dad lay. Sometimes the night ended in tears, my running over to his gravestone.

Was Velma in New Jersey around her "Dead Mom Day"? Was she pummeled by grief, being back where she had lived her first fourteen years with her mother? Was she missing the babies she had given up for adoption? I can imagine her, depressed and angry, at her grand-mother's home. There is no mention of alcohol in the summary, but was Velma coping with sadness by drinking heavily? If yes, did her grief and drinking combine into anger? My grief for my father didn't go to anger, but then, I hadn't also lost an anticipated sibling when Dad died. I hadn't given up two babies. If I even imagine losing one of my boys, my brain starts to unhinge. I can't go there.

She did.

Twice.

In Velma's day, unmarried women were not expected to have babies. Nor were women expected to remain unmarried. Velma did not follow the rules.

I was born the complacent, quiet, middle child, the straight A student, the serious gymnast, the one who skipped her last year of high school.

During my freshman year at Mount Holyoke College, I wrote dutifully to my parents, but my mother usually replied for both of them. Once, I wrote to my father at work, hoping he might answer. His response, the only letter I ever got from him, was classically "Dad." I left the box behind and went upstairs to find Dad's letter, wanting first to reread his words before I could face his mother's.

9/23/77

Dear Pam,

I received your letter this morning, & I guess you shamed me into writing a note. I am glad to hear that everything is A-OK at

School. You've got to remember that you are now in a different ballgame @ Mt. Holyoke. Your mother & I have the greatest confidence in you, & we know that you will be able to cope with any problem that may arise.

Not quite, Dad, not quite.

Jay started Hockey on Monday evening. He has 4 successive tryouts, & after the last one, 2 teams (A & B) are chosen. He will have no problem in making the "A" team this yr. Last night he beat supposedly the best player in his age group skating up & down the ice. Being somewhat biased, it looks as if he is one of the fastest on skates. He seems to be much stronger than last yr. It must be the weights.

How is gymnastics going? I think the weight program they have put you on will help tremendously with your stamina. Let us know what the gymnastic schedule will be.

Dad was a multiple sport athlete, a coach for youth sports in town, and a jogger. He encouraged us to be involved in sports. When I was young, I felt left out of things because I was awful at all the Dad-sports—soccer, baseball, basketball. Gymnastics helped me feel like I belonged in my family. What about Velma? Did sports matter at all in her life before Pilgrim State?

I hope you & Jamie enjoyed yourselves in Vermont this past weekend. Jamie's accounting course looks like a tough one. I told him the other night that it is important that he learn the fundamental acctng rules early, because if he doesn't, he will have a problem throughout the course.

Jamie was my boyfriend in high school and on into college. At the time we were involved, Jamie's dad was struggling with alcoholism. My dad had stepped in and played the father role many times—helping

Jamie get a part-time job and a car, and Dad was tutoring him in his early weeks at Western New England College.

It is now 1 o'clock in the afternoon, & I have got many things to do. I have been writing this on company time.

Have fun – See you soon,

Love Dad

Sixteen months after that letter, during my sophomore year, on January 19th, 1979, Dad would come home from playing basketball, walk to the refrigerator, and drop on the kitchen floor. Dead. He was forty-one. I was eighteen.

I returned to school after winter term on autopilot. For several semesters, I was able to keep up my grades, despite a lack of discipline in my studies and an increasing devotion to partying. During the second semester of my senior year at Mount Holyoke College, the sadness that I'd been avoiding with heavy drinking after Dad's death caught up with me. I didn't know how to live in a world without him. Unlike many fathers of the seventies, he showed up for everything. If I had a gymnastics meet coming that he couldn't make due to a meeting, he might pop in to a practice. He coached, encouraged, and bragged about me and my siblings. Maybe his omnipresence had something to do with being given up for adoption. There could never, ever be a question that he loved us.

I flunked out, the goody-two-shoes, born rule-follower. Twenty years old, in what should have been my last year of college, grief and purposelessness left me drunk often, hung over often, sad often, having meaningless sex often, and giving serious consideration to killing myself.

Maybe Velma was trying to get pregnant as a way to die and join her mother?

Did she lie awake hoping that she'd die in childbirth like her mother had?

I lay awake one night in my room in North Rockefeller Hall the spring I should have been looking forward to graduating. My hedonistic lifestyle and irresponsibility toward classwork meant there could be no last minute opportunity to finish papers, to pass exams — I had let everything go too far.

How could I go home and face my mother?

I couldn't even face myself in the mirror.

Maybe I should kill myself.

For that long, long night, I wrestled with the idea.

I wasn't at a point in my life where I believed in God — I had closed the door on even the possibility of a higher power when Dad died. There would be no prayers offered that night, none in the traditional sense.

Instead I wept. Piles of damp, rumpled tissues covered my floor. In the dark corner, leaning into my pillow, I said to no one, or to my guardian angels, "Okay, how?"

I had some Tylenol but wasn't sure that swallowing a half bottle of that would actually kill me. If I was going to do this, I wanted to be sure to die.

I could jump from the top floor of one of the dorms, but none of them seemed quite high enough to guarantee death.

Did they lock the kitchen? Could I stab myself with one of the kitchen knives? Then, I thought of my friends on the floor and how traumatizing it might be for one of them to find me. That wasn't fair; what a crappy thing to do to your friends right before graduation.

And then, I thought about my mother, sister, and brother. My life didn't feel like it mattered to me, but what about them?

Somewhere in my heart a little voice spoke the truth.

You do matter to them, even if you think you shouldn't.

That little voice carried a glimmer into the room.

A tiny spark.

Hope.

I would have to live, face what I had done and go on.

And, I did.

I lived through my suicide night.

Then, in my final weeks at Mount Holyoke, I met the man I would marry. I left school and moved in with my mother briefly and started working temp jobs. One of those temp jobs became a good "real" job at the *Wall Street Journal*. I worked there for a year, got married, and finished my last year of college at Wesleyan University, where my husband was a Visiting Assistant Professor. For me, "Considering Suicide Night" was a turning point — not that my grief was erased, or my bouts with depression were gone, but I believed I would find a way to make my life a good one, a life that mattered.

Velma hadn't reached her turning point yet on her visit to New Jersey. She may have had some sparks of hope left. How I wish I had a letter she'd written about this time, but her letters don't begin until after she was at Pilgrim State in 1947. I'm left to conjecture.

When she visited her grandmother, maybe she encountered a strict *oma* imposing a curfew. Perhaps twenty-nine-year-old Velma had reached the end of her ability to behave properly and follow the rules. I doubt she knew rebelling and acting up could land her in a hospital. She may not have known of the long tradition of women committed to psychiatric hospitals for dubious reasons. Before the 1940s and well after, husbands had wives committed and would then divorce them to marry someone else. Fathers had daughters committed. "Neurasthenia" diagnoses were the precursor to "nervous breakdown," both of which led to women being committed and never released. Nervous breakdown is not an accepted medical term. It is often used by the public to discuss acute stress disorder, panic attacks, schizophrenia, or post-traumatic stress disorder. It is not hard to imagine these diagnoses applying to Velma.

I once worked in public relations at Milwaukee (now Aurora) Psychiatric Hospital, helping research for the hospital's one hundredth anniversary celebration in 1984. Some of the small buildings on campus had been built by wealthy families to care for their daughters following mental breakdowns. Think of the famous example of Rosemary Kennedy, whose father agreed to doctors' recommendations that the "hard to manage" twenty-three-year-old Rosemary be given a new procedure, a lobotomy: a neurosurgical procedure severing connections in the brain's prefrontal lobes. After Rosemary's lobotomy in 1941, she was eventually moved to St. Coletta's in Jefferson, Wisconsin, where the Kennedy family built a home for her.

There would be no private home for Velma. Her father was not a wealthy man. Velma would be one of many patients, some sources say fourteen thousand, at Pilgrim State, which offered over-crowded, dismal conditions. And psychiatric treatment in the 1940s did not include the arsenal of medications that would become available a short decade later.

❖ ❖ ❖

Finally, I read her letters.

For her first several years at Pilgrim State, Velma writes like any sane person. She asks about her daddy, Gram, her brother. She misses them on holidays, birthdays, and funerals. She often reassures Gram, *"Don't fret or worry about me. I'm fine."* The madwoman ravings come later, interspersed with normal letters.

She talks about her care in language that sounds like it was written a few days ago, instead of many decades ago.

> *Today we had shock treatments again and boy, it knocked me for a loop. I don't know why...*

> *Dear Everyone, I was told today that I'm all through with treatments and will go home in perhaps about two weeks. I was so happy.*

But two years later:

> *Next Sunday I hope to be released and I hope you'll get here as specified... I'll be so happy to get out and live again, God only knows.*

Many of her notes are neatly written in tiny script, using every available quarter inch on small, lined post cards, the way nine-year-old me wrote in my tiny diary. She loves the visits every two weeks, one hour on Sundays, from Aunt Millie and her cousin, Mildred. She requests things: *"Bring me another Dr. Lyon's toothpaste on Sunday, please. Cigarettes too, you know when I get out I'll make it up to you both."*

As 1950 began, three years into her stay, she wrote to her father and stepmother: *"Dear Abby + Daddy, ... I'm so glad the holidays are over but now to pull thru Jan 4th to 9th — you know how I go to pieces home but I'll do my best here."*

My heart sinks.

She is referring to her tendency to "go to pieces" at home each year around the time of her mother's death. She did suffer around the time of "Dead Mom Day."

Three years into her stay in some of her letters her agitation is visible — her penmanship loosens up. Spacing between words increases. She stops filling every possible space on the line even though paper is precious. Angry at Aunt Mildred — one of her only visitors — for some unexplained slight, she writes, the letters dark and firm: *"Are you aware of the fact that this is going to end up in a Federal or State Court Room? You are both involved, but it's your choice and far be it from me to try to change your minds."*

Her sense of hygiene is important. She complains about the *filthy people* there. I have not been able to find any photographs of the washrooms at Pilgrim State, but they were likely communal. Also, some of the residents may not have been able to tend to their own hygiene. With over fourteen thousand patients at times, the staff probably couldn't keep up. I'm sure there were many filthy people there.

Besides writing paper and three-cent stamped envelopes, she often asks for Woodbury soap, ten-cent-size Maybelline black mascara, bobbie pins, hairnets, Burry's crackers, peanut butter and jelly. She keeps busy crocheting and reading, and asks for needles, thread, books, magazines like *Life* and *Time*.

Life. Time. She has no control over either in her life at Pilgrim State.

I read and search, but find only two references to my father. In a letter dated February 6th, his birthday, she writes, *"Jon, je ne vais jamais t'oublier."* "Jon, I'll never forget you." Her handwriting is light. Have I read it correctly? It is inserted between requests for things—a tiny foreign moment.

Pourquoi en français? Je ne sais pas.

Her father was German, yet she had studied French. I suppose, in the post-World War I era, when she was in high school, many Americans of German ancestry might have opted to study something other than German.

I studied French and have loved it—the language, the culture, the country. A tenuous connection, *certainement*, but it's something.

I search for any other connection, however tenuous, beyond biology, but at the same time, biology won't be denied. Her sad young face in that black and white photo I'd seen looked an awful lot like me. I suspect the photo was taken after her mother's death, but before Velma's pregnancies. She may be sixteen or seventeen. She has the lost look of a motherless young woman.

She doesn't realize that she has so much more to lose.

❖ ❖ ❖

I can't stop thinking of her at age nineteen and then twenty, pregnant and unmarried. I was nineteen within six months of my dad's death, drowning my tears in bottles of Miller beer.

Why no shotgun wedding when she was pregnant with my father? Why another baby, a little over a year later, another boy, also given up for adoption? Again, why no wedding? Wouldn't a wedding have been typical in the forties? She moved to the D.C. area sometime after the second birth and worked as a nurse's aide. Why D.C.? Why so far from family and friends? Then, that visit to her grandmother in New Jersey, that "spell," and on to Bellevue and then Pilgrim State.

I'm trying, trying to understand the turn of her life, trying to connect to something, anything. But the thing I see that we share the most is the loss of a parent in our youth.

For years, my life was divided into two parts: when Dad was alive and when he wasn't. My drinking, pot-smoking, and squandering of time and money weren't uncommon in the 1970s, so I could hide my grief — until I couldn't anymore. In American culture, then and now, it was more acceptable to be drunk than to be grieving.

Love of and from my family, my birth family, and my new family with my husband, all that love saved me. Growing up and realizing that I wanted to live a life that would honor my father's legacy saved me.

Velma had lost so much more. When her mother died, she lost both her mother and an anticipated younger sibling. When her father took a job in Massachusetts, she lost the community and family she knew. By her mid-twenties, she already seemed destined for prolonged sadness. A dead mother and sibling. A new community. Two babies given away. But things got worse, much, much worse.

❖ ❖ ❖

The box holds a letter dated March of 1950. The letter was sent to Velma's father from Harry J. Worthing, M.D., Senior Director at Pilgrim:

Dear Sir:

I am writing to you concerning your daughter, Velma Gasteyer, now a patient in Building 6 of this hospital.

Her condition during the last month has shown no improvement and she has developed tendencies which require a consideration of some further procedure in her case.

Her imaginations have become much more vivid and she feels herself threatened. She has been carefully examined and the operation of prefrontal lobotomy has been recommended in her case....

Twelve days later, her father responds, also in a typed letter:

My dear Doctor Worthing: —

Thank you for your letter of March 10th concerning my daughter, Velma Gasteyer.

Due to the fact that I am in very poor physical health my doctor advises that I do not make the trip to the hospital at Brentwood. We know that Velma is in good care and that you all are doing everything possible to make her well.

My sister, Mrs. Waterfield will be at the hospital Sunday April 2nd and will try to see Dr Brill between 2 and 5 p.m. In the meanwhile I am returning the Surgical or Treatment Permit, signed by me and 2 witnesses, so that you can proceed with the operation of prefrontal lobotomy which you recommend. After the operation I would like to be advised of just what the future holds for Velma....

The tone of her father's letter reflects the reality of the time. People did not question medical authorities the way we are encouraged to in the twenty-first century. I've needed three surgeries in the past eight years, a lumpectomy, a hysterectomy, and a meniscus repair. In all cases, I asked questions, sought information, and was in charge of my care. Velma's care options were not hers to consider.

The late 1940s and early 1950s have been called the heyday of lobotomies in the United States. The earliest lobotomies were performed with ice picks. Velma landed at the center of the lobotomy craze. An estimated two thousand Pilgrim State patients were lobotomized at that time. In a paper in the *American Journal of Psychiatry* in 1951, Pilgrim State doctors Worthing, Brill, and Wigderson wrote about a study of their lobotomy patients:

A very important effect of the operation, behavior improvement, developed in even the most chronic cases although in smaller proportion than in less chronic ones. Approximately two-thirds of all operated cases remaining in the hospital showed material improvement in such behavior disorder as aggressiveness, destructiveness, wetting, soiling, homosexual behavior on a psychotic level, refusal of food, etc. After a period of post-operative observation that now ranges from 1 to 4 years, it appears that approximately one-third of all operated cases have been able to return to their homes and to remain there.

Was Velma part of that study? What really led to the recommendation of the lobotomy? Had she refused food? Had she behaved aggressively? Only one-third of those cases returned home and remained there; yet the procedure continued.

Pre-frontal lobotomies did not always turn victims into complete vegetables, zombies like McMurphy in *One Flew Over the Cuckoo's Nest*. These crude operations damaged different parts of the brain. Outcomes varied significantly.

❖ ❖ ❖

I spend several days fighting day-mares of icepicks, split brains, and my biological grandmother, not yet thirty years old, clear-headed and brain not yet divided.

I want to hold her, to give her hope. I want to murder the doctor who recommended the lobotomy. I want to scream at her father — my great-grandfather — "Don't do it. Don't let them do this."

But the deal is done and the box remains. I can only hold copies of her letters.

My head aches, deep and insistent, as if it will split.

❖ ❖ ❖

After the lobotomy, Velma wasn't a vegetable. She continued to write letters after her "procedure." Some are clear — asking for things, thanking for visits — but others mark a shift.

Dear Daddy and Abbie,

Those planes overhead are for my protection. At night, there are about 25 or 30, they make stars and some use metal tile practicing psychology.

Dear Mildred,

My son, Jonathan, has been in hospital twice in the past two weeks. His head has almost been cut off from two morons. One female, one male.

Dear Gram,

Trust you all are fine. I'm not exactly well but I don't give a damn. I'm leaving today at 4:12 pm for Washington, DC. Did you know I'm a registered geologist?

Dear Mildred:

How is Kitty? Tell her tomorrow I'm pulling out for 19th Street and 7th Avenue. Love always, Queen Velma Claire.

❖ ❖ ❖

In 1952, her letters stop. Perhaps she didn't stop writing them, but the recipients (Aunt Millie and Mildred) no longer could stand to keep them.

From the hospital, in 1962, there's notice of a fight. A coat hanger. A need for eye surgery.

A coat hanger. Eye surgery. I squeeze my eyes shut.

Nothing more but her death certificate. She died in late 1980, when I was twenty. She died after Dad did, when I was nearing my suicide contemplation night. She wasn't yet sixty-three years old. She'd been in the hospital for thirty-three years — more than half her life.

The unfairness makes my head pound.

I close the box and my eyes. She outlived my father.

She never knew what a good man he was. She never knew that

her baby, Jon Gasteyer, was raised as James Parker in Southampton, Massachusetts.

❖ ❖ ❖

I didn't know what I would find in the box; I only know the feelings I wrestle with now. How cheated she was. Her mother and sibling gone, her babies gone and then her life, thirty-three years in a nightmarish hospital.

I used to think Dad was cheated, dying before he reached his forty-second birthday, but compared to his mother, he had a good life. He raised three children. He was loved and worked hard, earning admiration and respect. A softball field in Southampton is named for him. His life efforts and values resonate through his grandchildren's lives, even though they never met him.

❖ ❖ ❖

I write a letter to her, using my neatest penmanship and reminding myself to sprinkle in some *Français,*

> *Dear Velma,*
>
> *I am one of your granddaughters, your Jon's second daughter. He was a good man, a wonderful man, and losing him was almost my undoing. I understand your sadness about your mother's death. Vraiment.*
>
> *You were born at the wrong time. I imagine you wanted things that weren't options in your time: independence, sex and love without marriage, and to be a single mother.*
>
> *You had every reason to be sucked into the darkness of depression. I know that dark place. But today, they don't lock us away and cut our brains if the depression curtain falls. Today there are pills I take for my sadness. They help me navigate the down times.*
>
> *I love many of the things you did: needlework, reading, French.*

*My sons. I have two sons also, your great-grandsons. They know
your story. You will not be forgotten.*

    All my love and kisses,
    Pamela xxxxxx

I kiss the letter, as I imagined she often did with hers, and place
it in the blue cardboard box.

Velma Gasteyer, 1951

RAMONA M. PAYNE has been a writer for years and her favorite form is creative nonfiction, particularly the personal essay. With a degree in liberal arts and an MBA, she left her career in corporate and nonprofit leadership to focus on her writing. A pivotal experience was completing the Creative Writing program at The University of Chicago Graham School.

Ramona considers reading, walking, and Pilates as essential practices for her writing. She lives in South Bend, Indiana, with frequent trips to Cincinnati, Ohio, and northern Virginia. She is currently working on a collection of essays and enjoys participating in writing workshops and conferences because they build community. Visit her website and blog at ramonapayne.com.

I wrote my essay, "Without Words," after discovering documents of a purchase that my husband's mother made many decades ago. We found them in a case that we received after her passing, and we were surprised by the information it contained. I chose these papers because they gave me insight into a woman that I never had the chance to know.

In life we often depend on spoken words to communicate with people, to understand them. By discovering these papers and doing additional research, I learned more about who my mother-in-law was as a younger woman. I believe that her purchase gave a glimpse of the kind of life she wanted to create, years before she had a husband and sons. This essay is one of many in a collection I am writing that explores how family artifacts and stories shape our understanding, traditions, and values.

BY RAMONA M. PAYNE

Without Words

I saw my mother-in-law Mary only twice before she died, and both times she did not speak to me. By the time I met her, Parkinson's had spirited away her ability to talk or smile. Each time I went to visit, she focused her intense dark eyes on me and I wondered, *what is she thinking?*

Tony and I began dating in our forties; we had known each other in college. He came from a small family; his father had died the year before we reconnected, and his mother was living in Colorado Springs, closer to his two brothers, Mike and Mark. I had seen photos of Mary — at San Francisco Giants games in later years, grinning with her husband, and as a young mother in fitted cotton dresses, tending to her three boys. From the beginning, I knew Tony was close to his mother. "I miss talking to her like we used to," he told me early in our relationship. He explained that because of her illness she was slowly losing her ability to speak.

His phone calls with her could seem one-sided, but I knew better. Tony would ask a question, and then there would be a long pause on his end while his mother responded. Tony was patient; he did not rush her, trying to fill in words that might take a while to come. A few months after we started dating, Tony and I attended the world premiere of the opera *Margaret Garner*; he was handsome in his blue suit, and I wore a dress in ombre shades from turquoise to indigo, with a lightly-sequined wrap to keep away the chill. Before we took our seats, he phoned his mother while I peered over the balcony to watch people arriving at the theatre.

"Mom, I'm at the opera with Ramona." He waited for what he knew would be a labored response, if she would be able to talk at all. Then came his laughter. "What did you say? You never liked opera? Well, I have never been to one before but I'm looking forward to it." There were a few more pauses while he let her take her time to finish their conversation. Then, "Okay Mom, I love you, bye." When he got off his cell phone he was smiling, despite how few words were exchanged. For a moment she was her former self, full of life and her strong opinions.

He turned to me and said, "Mom tried opera once and didn't like it."

I laughed. "Well, opera is an acquired taste," I said, "but if you pick the right opera, everyone can find one they like." That was May and by fall she could no longer speak.

We planned a trip to Colorado, and he tried to prepare me for a visit that would involve very little conversation. I assumed that I would come up with some way to communicate with her. I found it easy to talk to people, even strangers, because I figured there is always a connection if you ask enough questions. Even if we could not talk to one another, maybe she would see something in me that was familiar. We were both dark-skinned, with a gap in our front teeth. She wore her hair in a short snow-white afro; my hair was also natural, but hung in locks that were starting to show gray.

Upon arrival, Tony spent time with his brother, and I tagged along on an errand with his wife. As it turned out, she decided to drop something off for Mary so we stopped by the assisted living facility, a well-maintained series of buildings situated in view of the Front Range of the Southern Rocky Mountains.

We made our way to Mary's floor, letting the staff know that we were looking for her. The introduction was brief: "Mom, this is Ramona; she is a friend of Tony's."

Did she wonder where Tony was? "Hi, it's nice to meet you," I said. I was surprised by how tiny she was and wished that she was able to flash the broad smile I had seen in pictures that Tony shared with me. I looked at her hands, which were settled in her lap. Tony once told me how my hands reminded him of his mother's, because of the way our long fingers held on firmly to another hand. Mary looked at me, and even though her movements were slight, I felt like she was looking me over, trying to discern if I was the right woman for her son.

Later I returned with Tony, his sister-in-law again leading the way. This time I took in the spacious lounge, a dining room that served as a gathering spot, the small yet tidy apartments for the residents. "There are more women than men here," I whispered to Tony. Many of the women still found the time for makeup or a quick smear of lipstick. Most women outlive their husbands. I thought about Tony and me; given our late start, would that be us? If we married, we might not have as many years together as our parents had.

We knocked on Mary's door; it was slightly open. Tony's mother, a small woman who seemed barely over five feet tall, sat bent over in a chair. I thought about the photos I had seen of her and expected her to be closer to my height, but she was at least three or four inches shorter. When she saw us, there was no verbal greeting, no wave of the hand, no hurried rush towards the door to hug her son, not even a tear of recognition. Mary fixed her eyes on Tony, glanced at me, and back at him. Her intense stare was balanced by her frailty and petite size, yet suddenly I felt awkward and shy. He walked over to her, bent over and held his mother. "I love you Mom." Leaning in close, he continued to speak to her, holding her hands.

"Mom, this is Ramona, I told you about her."

I said hello and smiled but realized this was not going as I expected. I was accustomed to using words to express how I felt, and questions helped me learn more about someone. Hugging her, when she could not express if this is what she wanted, seemed inappropriate.

"Mom, would you like to show us around this place?" Tony asked. "I want to see your friends from bingo, the ones you always beat when you play." The residents often made sure their friends who lived there knew when they had visitors. Having company was not only a comfort; it was a matter of pride. Using a walker, she led us around the building as if to say, *Look, they came to see me. These are the people who love me.* She took her time, lingered in a hallway, or looked around and waited for her friends to yell out, "Hello Mary, is that your son?" She could not smile or respond, "Yes, this is my son and his friend." She kept the same fierce unchanging look, but we knew she was happy to have company.

On both days of our visit, I spoke very little because our time was brief and I could see her focus was on Tony. I did not want to appear like I was prattling on, interrupting the precious time they had together. Tony had been warned that she would want to leave the building when it was time for him to go, and it was true — parting was difficult for both of them. At the end of the visit he reached for his mother's hand and they walked outside. Tony slowed his pace while she shuffled next to him. "I love you Mom," was all that he said. One more word and the tears settling in his eyelids would have spilled over. She looked at him, her eyes fixed on his, grasping his hand yet unable to ask him to stay a bit longer. This was the last time I saw them together. She clung to him; he was torn between staying and prolonging a difficult goodbye.

I have always wondered what was going on behind her eyes. Later I felt like I should have hugged her or told her how much I loved her son. These are the things I might have done if there had been more back and forth, a conversation that extended beyond glances. I wondered if she approved of me, if she could see that Tony was happier than he had been in years. A year or so later Tony rushed out to see his mom when she became very ill. He said he sat with her, holding her hands and telling her how much he loved her. "I let her know that I'm good, I'm happy and in love, that she doesn't need to worry about me. I told her that I know she's tired and misses Dad, and it is okay." It was not long after his visit that she passed away.

❖ ❖ ❖

Months after her death, Tony's brother Mark sent us a grayish-brown leather case; in it was his mother's silver service. Tony opened the case and, except for some tarnish, the silverware was in good condition. He placed it on a shelf in our bedroom closet, where it remained untouched for a couple of years.

One day in early fall I mentioned the silver. "We really should take a look at it," I said. "I can probably find a polish or something to clean it."

"Hmm, that would be nice, we might as well use it." Tony said.

We had never really examined the contents. He went into the closet and pulled the case down, and we sat on our bed to open it. Inside was a complete sterling silver service, with special forks, knives, and serving utensils. The pieces had a decorative pattern at the top, a design of flowers and swirls, lily-like flourishes and tendrils. It was in great condition, with only a hint of tarnish that gentle cleaning would easily remove. I imagined the dinners where it was used, the setting of many tables for holiday meals, his mother watching her husband and three boys eat the food she had prepared with love. After dinner, Mary would have washed the forks and knives, and then dried each piece by hand before gently placing it in her case until the next formal event.

I saw folded pieces of paper in the case, one sheet that had shipping instructions and another blue sheet that looked like a receipt. There was handwriting on the back; on the front in bold capital letters were the words "The Most Important Thing About Sterling and China Is Getting Started."

"Tony look, your mom got her silverware in Chicago. The receipt says that the Easterling Silver Company is on Wells Street."

Mary was born in Georgia in 1927, two years prior to the Great Depression. A silver service would have been a luxury then—perhaps it also was when she bought it as an adult. She served in the U.S. Army as a nurse, where she met her husband, Tony's father, and they married in October 1956. I looked over the Easterling receipt; it indicated that she bought the silver in 1954.

"She bought this before she got married," I said. I liked this, her independence; she probably made this decision before she met Tony's father. After Mary graduated from nursing school, she left the familiarity of her home in the South to join the military, eventually living abroad in Japan at a time when few other women, especially black women, were traveling around the world to serve. It must have taken as much courage and independence to leave the United States as it did to move away from her family home. Then, from a meager military salary of three hundred and forty dollars, she paid $21.65 towards the balance each month, information that the Easterling saleswoman had written on her contract.

"That's Mom's handwriting," he said, looking at the back of the receipt that showed a balance declining with each payment.

The more I studied the paper and the more I touched the silver, the more Tony's mother came alive for me. Mary, who could not tell me her stories in her own voice, spoke to me through what she left behind.

Easterling silver came from the name for silver coins, which the Germans called Easterlings. These coins were widely accepted as a standard of English currency. This name was eventually abbreviated to Sterling, which is now used to refer to the highest grade of silver metal. The Easterling Company offered a plan where women could pay for their silver service over time, through monthly installments. In Mary's time, some girls would have prepared for marriage by starting a hope chest, which contained the items used to set up a home. Mary must have had a vision for her life as a professional woman, one that started before her husband and sons became a part of it. Did the numerous moves required by a life in the military, to Alaska, Germany and various parts of the States, allow her to entertain in the ways she must have dreamed when she purchased such beautiful silver? The name of her silver pattern is Southern Grandeur. I wondered if she liked the name as much as the design, if it may have reminded her of her southern heritage and Georgia. I wondered what it must have been like to have only boys later, and no daughters with whom she could share the silver and housekeeping tips on how to properly set a table.

❖ ❖ ❖

My vision of Mary preparing the meal for her family becomes complete. I see her seated at a well-appointed dinner table with five place settings of silver, ready to receive the meal she has prepared for her husband and three sons. They pray before the meal, and I am certain that the ones grasping her hands on either side can feel her love and respect. They, in turn, send that love back to her. She is happy to have made such a spread. The sounds of talking and laughter fill the room as they sit around the table.

Tony tells me a joke that he and his mother once shared. She asked him, "If you were running down the street naked, and could cover just one part of your body, what part would you choose?" I laugh right away at the thought of Tony and his mom sitting together and her opening with what sounds like a bawdy joke.

"This is my mom," Tony says to me. "So I'm wondering where she is going with this. I tell her, I don't know, what part would you cover? 'My face,' she says." Tony and I fall over in laughter.

I wonder what our conversations would be like if she were still alive and hosting family dinners. But I realize that there is more than one way to get behind those eyes, to know the woman. Her treasures stowed away tell part of her story. Her eyes, fixed on Tony, were one way to communicate when she was alive. Her touch, her hand clasping Tony's hand as they said goodbye, was another. Spoken words are not the only way to come to know someone. There are times when instead of talking or questioning or focusing on making myself known, I must observe and listen, open the case, hold the silver, and imagine.

VALERIE REYNOLDS has always been a letter writer — to family and friends, to her four daughters when they were away at college, Round Robin letters with a circle of high school friends years later. When she retired from her secretarial job (where she wrote business letters all day long), a writer friend gave her a journal which she's been keeping since 1984. That was also the year she had her first grandchild, and now all nine of them enjoy her stories about themselves as they were growing up. Valerie loves her Writers' Club at Harwood Place where she is still writing.

My husband's mother saved every letter he wrote to his family when he was in the Army in World War II, from basic training to life in a foxhole. I put them in two scrapbooks and added the ones he wrote to me. It is from these books I wrote this piece.

BY VALERIE REYNOLDS

She Wrote a Good Letter

S he sat at the dining room table on a Sunday afternoon. The smell of coffee and bacon came in waves and the dishes were in the sink. Mom must have been in a hurry to get on the road with the rest of the family to visit her sister in the TB San where she'd been in and out for years. She had decided not to go this time, to fulfill a promise she'd made to her friend Nancy, a promise to write a letter to Nancy's older brother, who was in the Army and stationed in Europe.

What should she write about? He'd played basketball in high school, so maybe he'd be interested in Friday's game score. But that might make him sad that he wasn't still on the team.

Not about his family — they wrote him often. His parents got up early enough to listen to the news on the radio before they left for work in defense factories, trying to figure out where his unit might be in action.

Not about new movies she'd seen. Not when he was living in foxholes.

Her Parker pen sat on the table near her right hand, the blank sheet of paper in front of her. Why hadn't she gotten a V-Mail from Nancy? V-Mails were very small, and she could easily fill one page. Well, she'd give it her best.

❖ ❖ ❖

Her folks had talked her out of going to Washington, D.C., to become a Government Girl to help with the War Effort—she was only seventeen. So the only "effort" she'd made was to buy stamps and war bonds. She got a job, typing Government orders with nine carbon copies (a pain to correct if you made an error). She'd researched airlines and found that Eastern required two years of college and two years of business experience of their stewardesses. She'd saved her money from her secretarial job, been accepted at a college; she was well on her way to becoming a stewardess—her dream come true! After the war, the new airline business should be booming.

In the meantime, writing letters to GIs might count a little toward the Effort. And she felt she owed Nancy and Nancy's mother, who'd asked her to write, too. She'd had dinners and stayed overnight a number of times at their home when the gang was doing something special, and she was always made welcome. She already wrote to a boyfriend, high school friends and cousins—all in the service. But she'd known them all and what they'd like to hear about: who was going with whom, who'd gone to college or was working (and where). She'd never met Nancy's brother.

❖ ❖ ❖

"I got a letter from Valerie," he wrote his family a couple of weeks later. "She seems like a nice kid. I'm glad she wrote, she writes a good letter."

To her, he wrote from his foxhole, "Good morning — it's raining but it's light enough to see to write." Thus began their regular correspondence.

He wrote about how they farmed in Europe. After all, she was a farmer's daughter. She asked him how the food was. He said it wasn't too bad.

He told about the clean factories in Belgium and how they'd let the GIs use their showers now and then.

She asked him if he planned to go on to school when he got home. He said yes, on the GI Bill. He wrote how lucky they were if the foxholes were dug by GIs who'd moved up to the line of battle.

She asked him if he'd like to travel after the war. He answered yes, he'd like to buy a good car and drive across the United States.

When he was discharged and came home, he took her out to thank her for her letters.

Two years later, they were wed, a marriage that would last for sixty-six years.

She wrote a good letter.

Jessica Schnur has a MA in English and Writing from Mount Mary University and a MFA in Fiction from the Solstice program at Pine Manor College. She currently teaches in the Humanities, Social Science, and Communication department at the Milwaukee School of Engineering. She writes fiction and non-fiction and her work has been published in the *Sheepshead Review, Door is a Jar,* and *Litbreak,* and she was a Wisconsin Writer's Association Jade Ring Award winner for non-fiction. She spends her free time reading and running many, many miles — she and her husband are trying to run a marathon in all fifty states.

When my mother died, I had to write a eulogy to give at the funeral. I was at a loss as to where to begin, so I asked some of my family members for their favorite memories of my mom. Several sent me emails that I used to help structure the original eulogy and then again when I rewrote it as this piece. At the funeral, we had a guestbook for people to write their favorite memory of my mom in as well. Some of these also inspired the spirit of the piece and helped to inspire a cleaner rewrite of the connections I made between my family members' memories and my own.

Schnur Family Announcement

For Release: 6:30 PM
May 21, 2014

THE SCHNUR FAMILY would like to thank you for taking the time to celebrate the life of an amazing wife, mother, grandmother, sister, aunt, and friend, Debbie. The amount of support has been overwhelming and indescribably appreciated.

Some of you have shared your stories about Debbie, and, throughout all of them, her charm, kindness, and wisdom were a common thread.

Even when she was very young, she was able to persuade her older brother and sister to do many things. One frequent activity was playing hide and seek. Bill and Pam would pretend that they didn't know that she had hidden inside the clothes hamper (again) and they would sit on the lid wondering aloud "where could Debbie be?" while this little muffled voice would say "I'm in here guys," louder and louder, until she was near tears...at which time they would jump up and pretend to be surprised that she had been in the hamper the whole time. One can only imagine the hamper had some sort of ventilation and thus was relatively safe—in sharp contrast to the alternative game in which Bill would hold her by her ankles over the ledge of the balcony, the third floor balcony.

Her persuasive powers continued into adulthood. One afternoon, Debbie offered to watch Natalie and Danny, her niece and nephew, so her sister-in-law, Sue, could get a haircut. Sue came back in tears because the stylist chopped her hair, and she was convinced she looked like a boy with a bad haircut. Soon Debbie had her laughing, and Sue almost forgot about her lack of hair. As they were getting ready to leave, Natalie said, "Mom, I still think you look pretty." Later, when they were in the car on the way home, Natalie said, "Mom, Debbie told me to say you looked pretty, but I think you look beautiful."

This wonderful story actually teaches us two things: it's always important to be kind, and Natalie's the one to seek out if you're afraid you've gotten a bad haircut.

Another niece, Jenny, spent a lot of time with Debbie and Debbie's daughter, Jessica, when Jenny and Jessica were young. They created great works of art, brewed leaf tea, swam in the pool of their apartment complex, and, the most fun of all, dressed up Debbie's cats in fancy outfits — which upset Debbie a little. One can't imagine why. Clearly the cats loved it.

It was during these times together that Debbie imparted sage wisdom on Jenny and Jessica. Jenny claims that it is because of Debbie that she has good dental hygiene. Debbie once yelled at them (but not harshly) for not flossing their teeth at night when Jenny slept over. Jenny felt horrible and didn't want to upset or disappoint her Aunt Debbie. From then on she flossed. Every night. She still does, and so does Jessica. Debbie also taught them that the miraculous way to make vegetables taste good was to put cheese on them. Perhaps this was the early push that led them both to become vegetarians later.

Along with sharing good dental hygiene and eating habits, Debbie encouraged them to face their fears. It is funny that Jenny remembers her first roller coaster ride was on the Tidal Wave at Great America. For those of you who do not remember or may not have had the pleasure of riding the Tidal Wave, it was powder blue, and fairly simple. Riders went through one loop, straight up, down, and back through the loop. Jenny became an instant roller coaster lover and rode a second time. In contrast, after Jessica was convinced to ride with her mom when she was five, she fainted before the first loop had even been completed, and Debbie had toothmarks on her arm where Jessica had bitten down in terror before she passed out.

It is impossible to pick only one or even a few memories that capture Debbie. She was beautiful, brilliant, stubborn, kind, strong, and dedicated. One could sit and list adjectives all night and it would not do her justice. After all, how can we capture the true essence of a person, a life, in a list?

Debbie and Mark dedicated every ounce of energy to making sure Joe, Jeremy, and Jessica had every opportunity in life. They pushed them to reach for their dreams, to put forth their best effort in everything they attempted. Debbie never went to college, but she placed a very high value on education. And she was very wise.

Debbie was sick for a long time, yet even after her tumor robbed her of her ability to work, drive, use her left hand, walk, and even speak, she refused to give up. She always believed there might be a chance she would get better. She continued physical therapy in hopes that she would somehow gain back some of the strength she had lost. As recently as five months ago, Jessica and Debbie were talking, and Debbie said "when I can walk again." Not if, *when*. This was after her most recent scan had shown that the tumor had become immune to chemo and could no longer be stopped. Even up until the very last week, when she couldn't speak at all, she would wave her arm to indicate she wanted to be pulled up into a standing position. Mark held her up and Jeremy was in charge of moving her feet — she still wanted to walk.

If Jessica were to choose only one memory of Debbie to share, it would be this.

She remembers a phone conversation she had with Debbie several years ago. Jessica hated her job, was struggling to finish a Master's program in education that she was not engaged or really interested in any longer. A stressful relationship was leaving her mentally and emotionally depleted. She remembers venting about all of the things wrong with her life and telling Debbie that she was stuck. Debbie immediately stopped Jessica and said emphatically: "You are never stuck. You can always choose something different, you can always choose a way out."

Her voice was firm, almost cold, and stopped Jessica's rant. And, in the months that followed, Jessica continued to think about what Debbie had said.

Jessica finished out the degree program, quit the suffocating job she hated and the relationship, too. She found enough part time and temporary work to get by, then enrolled in a graduate writing program. Once Jessica had done all of these things, she found many of her other problems resolved themselves. She slept well.

Debbie was right. Jessica wasn't really stuck. She had just convinced herself that she was. Debbie might say, even now, we are often our own worst enemy when it comes to trapping our minds in the realm of *I can't*. But we can always change our lives, regardless of our situation. We always, always, always have a choice. Because our lives will never be perfect. And if we spend them waiting for the right time to be happy, or to make a change, or to do the things we want to do, we will wait forever.

We make the choice to walk.
To walk away.
To walk back.
To walk toward what terrifies us or what brings us comfort.
Toward love or solace.
Pleasure or pain.
The places we end up are our own.
It is never too late to walk somewhere new.
We are never stuck.

# # #

MEAGAN SCHULTZ lives in Milwaukee, Wisconsin, with her husband and two young boys, where she writes between naps with reheated coffee. She mostly finds herself musing on motherhood and midlife in the Midwest. Her work has appeared on *Literary Mama*, *Write On, Mamas*, and the *Brain, Child* blog, "Brain, Mother," and she is a contributing writer for the MKE Moms Blog and Lake Effect on 89.7 WUWM. She keeps up her own personal blog at www.meaganschultz.com when the laundry is finished (which is to say about once a week).

I often wonder how my children will remember me. I don't mean for what I've done, or the lessons I'll have passed on to them. I mean what image will be etched into the backs of their eyelids when they close their eyes and remember their mother. Will it be a grey-haired, wrinkly woman with deep set crow's feet from years of laughing? Will it be a pudgy-bellied, varicose-veined, watery-eyed old lady whose hands are at once paper thin and leathered? I hope so.

At the same time, I wish for them to remember me exactly as I am today at forty-one. The grey hairs are creeping slowly, and only occasionally do I reach for my ten-dollar readers when I squint at the paper. I am quite certain this is the me I will always feel I am. I hear my grandmother laughing at such naïveté. But I am fascinated by this idea of how we will be remembered and who we are at our core.

This is probably why I was so keen to document this story of my grandparents' letters. To see them through these love notes is to see them as entirely different but incredibly real human beings. I describe them as "The Bickersons," and indeed, if you had met them, you would understand that this term is not an understatement. But I would be remiss if I didn't also tell how much love there was, once.

Perhaps this is why fairy tales always begin "Once upon a time." Because this "once" is somewhere we all wish to remember. After four children, nine grandchildren, and six great-grandchildren, will we all remember that once upon a time, our grandparents knew love? If for nothing else, I want their descendants, my family, to see that it was real.

BY MEAGAN SCHULTZ

They Were Young Once, Too

"We wanted you to have these," the note said when I opened the package from my grandparents. Buried beneath the Styrofoam peanuts and crumpled newspaper was a tattered Christmas box with faded red stripes from an old Toledo department store of a bygone era. I looked down at the small box, wondering what my grandmother could possibly be sending me now. She had already given me her wedding photos, my father's senior class portrait (the last time we would see him without a mustache), old newspaper clippings from my parents' honeymoon spent hitchhiking around Europe, and boxes and boxes of square photographs with rounded edges.

"I'm only sharing them with you, I don't want anyone else to see them," she said when I called to let her know the package had arrived.

"We're getting on, and it's hard for us to read them anymore." She was referring to her eyesight. Once a year, she and my grandfather opened this box and reread the love letters they had written during their courtship in the early 1940s: torn scraps from notebooks, loose leaf pages from a school binder, and formal stationery, all stuffed carefully into a box that held the unfolding story of romance between two starry-eyed, love-struck teens.

❖ ❖ ❖

Author's grandfather

I know their story by heart. Downtown Toledo, 1943. It's raining "pitchforks and hammer handles" as my grandfather would say. He owns a Model A Ford and is driving his friends Bob and Jeannie to school when they see a girl standing against a building with an arm-load of books. She wears a crisp white uniform, a black raincoat, and a babushka on her head. "Why don't you go and ask her if she'd like a ride," my grandfather says to Jeannie, who goes to school with this girl. Of course the girl accepts.

As my grandmother tells it, he was going with someone else at the time and she wouldn't have dreamed of breaking them up. Unless she'd had to. And she *had* to, she says. She also never fails to mention that he made her pay for gas that day. They married six years later on a cool October afternoon.

❖ ❖ ❖

I couldn't decide whether I ought to read the letters. It seemed so personal, so intimate. Each yellowing paper folded into the tiniest square, creases worn from many readings over the years. I thought about my own love letters, the ones I'd scribbled to boys in my youth, before I had settled into my skin. Would I want my grandchildren reading them one day? Would I want them knowing my most urgent teenage desires? I dreaded to think of what my own letters must have said. And here I'd been given the chance to read theirs. I wondered if they'd be the same. One by one, I unfolded my grandparents' letters and peered into their world like a nosy neighbor.

❖ ❖ ❖

Though I grew up in California, I spent summers in Ohio with my grandparents. I was the first grandchild, the one they had grown to adore before my parents moved us out west like so many other long-haired hippies were doing in the mid-seventies, stuffing all our belongings in a U-Haul and heading for the Pacific. I didn't much care for California at first and spent the school years counting the days until summer vacation. Come June, I was the prodigal princess returned, to be spoiled as only grandparents can. My grandfather would spend all day at the family business he'd started with his father after World War II, and my grandmother would spend her days doting on me and making sure meals were ready when he got home (though really this only meant choosing which restaurant we'd eat out at or pick up from, as she'd given up her pots and pans when her last child moved out years earlier). I knew them then only as my grandparents. The two people who loved me more than anyone (except maybe my own parents), and who stood at the gate waving to me as I ran towards them from the plane every June.

❖ ❖ ❖

I blushed at the first letter. There, in the very same penmanship I would recognize anywhere from birthday cards and the weekly letters she used to send, was my young grandmother: *Honey, I love you with all my heart. Every time I think about the way you kissed me Sunday after-noon at Fallen Timbers, I get weak in the knees. I love when you kiss me so manly and surprisingly ... honey your [sic] really a dream boat.* Sitting at my dining room table, unfurling these letters littered with *"honeys"* and *"sweethearts"* and *"my darlings,"* I couldn't help but smile.

❖ ❖ ❖

Though never quite reaching five feet tall, my grandmother was a proud woman who stood her ground and made her presence known wherever she went. But never as much as she did on the dance floor. It was she who taught me to waltz, cha cha, and polka. She'd twist to tighten the reels of music for their player piano, slip the clasp onto the hook, and away the paper would spin. For the first few discordant notes we would steady ourselves in the living room, raising our elbows and assuming our position, and when the music began, we would dance. Oh how we would dance. It might have been "Down By The Old Mill Stream" or "The Entertainer" or "Never on a Sunday." It didn't matter, we loved them all. And when my grandfather came home, we would start again, this time with his tentative falsetto sing-song voice quivering in my ear and his cigar breath tickling my nose. "Put your arms around me, honey," he'd sing in his best Glenn Miller as he pulled me towards him, my head resting on his soft, round belly, his hands guiding me gently through the dance.

❖ ❖ ❖

He says, *Honey...you are different than I am. You like to live a fast life and you like to have fun and I just like to see a good cowboy or Indian show once in a while...I guess I'm a little old fashioned, I just dream about having a wife and some kids.*

She says, *I think a ranch style house would be cute after we had everything fixed up. We'll have a special place where you can keep your tools and I hope we can fix up a recreation room in the basement. I'm going to try to get a big can or something that we can put our money in. The first baby we have if it's a boy we'll name him Wayne. Wayne sounds pretty nice doesn't it???*

❖ ❖ ❖

By the time I came along, they'd moved out of the ranch home and into a two-story house they built in a new post-war sprawling neighborhood that backed onto a creek (which everyone pronounced *crick).* Thick, red shag carpet and olive green appliances offset the black and gold lamé wallpaper and crystal chandeliers that dripped like diamonds. My grandfather's company was doing well, and my grandmother was not afraid to spend the money he brought home. She enjoyed this newfound affluence that would come to define her as a modern wife and the well-heeled and much-envied den-mother of the block. She raised four children with little help from my grandfather, whose hours kept him at his tool plant long past bedtime, so little guilt would follow her spending. She would spoil three boys and a girl. Dwight (not Wayne) was the oldest, my father.

❖ ❖ ❖

If the letters were heavy with sickly sweet endearments, they were also clouded with the flip side of a new romance: jealousy. Apologies came frequently and self-deprecation filled pages. *I'm sorry, but it's because I love you so much that I get jealous,* or some version therein. It was mostly my grandmother apologizing for her envy and my grandfather apologizing for things he'd done to upset her. She worried when he talked to other girls, when he went to the pictures with his friends, when he hadn't written, when he forgot to call. *Darling please don't stop loving me,* she often begged. *I would marry you this minute if I could.*

My grandfather writes, *I hate to do things like that to you* [he was late], *you wouldn't understand, I'm not like the average boy, the circumstances with me are a little different, but I guess you'll have to put up with me. I don't know if you realize those things or not, but maybe you will some day.*

❖ ❖ ❖

"Some day" has come and is nearly gone. They've downsized from the two-story dream house, back to a ranch house, and now to a cramped two-bedroom apartment with nurses who knock each morning with pills and help my grandfather pull up his socks.

❖ ❖ ❖

Everything I'm living for now is for our future together. Every little thing I do now; such as sewing, washing, ironing, etc., I make believe it's your things and my things that I'm doing. You probably don't think anything of it when I wash your hankies but honey it means a lot more to me than you think it does.

She wanted to take care of him more than anything in the world. In 1949, they married and her dream came true.

❖ ❖ ❖

He jokes that around the senior community where they live, people call them "The Bickersons," a reference to an old radio comedy sketch show about a married couple who spend their waking hours at each other's throats in unrelenting squabble. This show aired first in September of 1946, at the height of my grandparents' adulation. Would they have been able to see themselves seventy years later? Would they recognize this couple who bark without the bite and bite without the sting? They, too, are relentless with their words, still profuse as ever, even if the banter they volley has long since changed.

❖ ❖ ❖

I can still smell summers with my grandparents. Whenever warm rain sizzles on the hot black asphalt, I always stop to inhale. I close my eyes and remember twirling up their driveway, leaping like a gazelle, partly because I believed I was Mary Lou Retton, but really because it was so hot beneath my feet I had no choice. Sometimes I sat at the driveway's edge on the warm grass and pushed my fingernails into the cracks of molten asphalt that felt like the puffy stickers I'd been collecting since the start of third grade. If I ran quickly, I'd make it to the backyard, where the patterned cement scratched like a pumice stone but at least didn't burn my toes, and into the pool to dive for the pennies my grandmother would throw in the deep end.

All my life they've spoiled me. I am as old as they were when I was born, with a husband and two boys of my own, and my grandmother still slips hundred-dollar bills in my pocket when I visit. "Treat yourself," she says, "and don't tell your grandfather I gave this to you. It's our secret." She won't let me refuse it. Nor will my grandfather, who slips me another bill on the way out the door.

But this box of letters is perhaps the greatest gift they've ever given me, the greatest secret I can never keep. In page after page of scribbled adoration, I see the meek and the messy, the ugly and the profane, but I am also privy to the beautiful and the wise, the mysterious and the sacred. In the beginning, it was a honeyed, innocent, tender love. And in the end, though drained of its saccharine, still love. Worn and weathered, but a love all the same. In the gift of these letters, I see myself. I see how it is I came to be, and how I am still becoming.

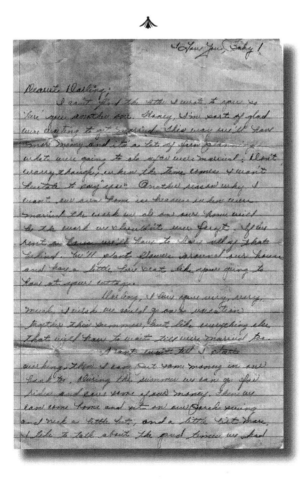

YVONNE STEPHENS lives with her husband and two children in Northwest Lower Michigan. She has worked as an assistant in the fields of mycology, forestry, and neurology research, volunteered for two years in the AmeriCorps, and most recently was an Artist Residency Coordinator for the Crosshatch Center for Art and Ecology. Yvonne is an award-winning poet, and was nominated for the Pushcart Prize in 2015. Her poems have appeared in the *Dunes Review* and the *LAND Creative Writing Journal.* Visit her blog at 40eyes.blogspot.com.

The poem "Syl" is from a letter my Grandfather wrote to my Grandmother (approximately 1950s).

The companion poem "Letters on Repeat..." is from a collection of letters exchanged between me and my Grandmother, Sylvia (Syl) between the years 1998 and 2007.

They are both found poems.

I didn't know my Grandmother very well as a child, and I never met my Grandfather

When I was in college, I began writing letters to my Grandmother. We developed a deep friendship through our writing. I would visit and stay with her in her apartment in Northern Michigan. She was a calming presence; always reassuring, and I loved listening to her stories. Her letters were gifts in the mail. Her handwriting is stunningly beautiful, and simply seeing the script on the page brings forth many memories and emotions.

She passed away shortly after I met my now husband, Jason. Her death was the first time I had lost someone I loved. In helping clear her apartment, I was gifted her sewing kit. The letter from my Grandfather was tucked inside, faded and worn.

She and my Grandfather met in high school in Hibbing Minnesota, were married in Detroit. They had a difficult marriage.

My father is the youngest of their five children, and I am his youngest daughter.

Syl

I will write a letter in a few days
to let you know what happens here
and what I will do.

Call Whitey and tell him
I will know something definite
in a couple days.

I guess
you have convinced my kids
I am nothing.

I borrowed again
to send this.
I don't have a cent.

Get a pair of shoes
for Pete
and buy groceries
for Hurleys.

Tell him
I will make it up to him
someday.

As ever

Al

"I will write a letter in a few days..."

BY YVONNE STEPHENS

Letters on Repeat from 728 W Spruce St.

for Sylvia

I was teasing when I called you crybaby.

I wanted to see you smiling & happy.
I used to cry too when I was young
even seeing road kill
or if someone teased me.

Sending you moola for a pizza 'on me.'
Life is what you make it,
ignore the snobs, they're only jealous
cuz of your smarts!!

Didn't sign the card
so you can re-use instead of re-cycle.
Love,
Your smart Grandma L.

I told Dr. I didn't want to live
to be 100 like my Ma.
He said it wasn't up to me.

Happy Valentine's Day!
The pup is so cute--
the verse stinks so ignore.

Your life now sounds like mine was--
bear, deer, Swan Lake & an outhouse.
A camp with a Finn sauna.

Gosh here I am 86 1/2 yrs. & still beefing.
I prayed for peace & quiet, I got it
but sometimes,
it gets to be a pain in the butt, toooo.

Joan called
when she got back home in Naples.
She said she just got out of the pool
& I told her she could stuff it.

There's an ole fart in apt. 14.
No matter when I go for mail
or take trash out, she's there.
I told her I didn't want her help
so I'm on the poop list.
It works~~

I was always a dickens,
& this slowing up gets me down.
But then the Sisu gets me out of that rut.

My ❤ problem can be scary at 93.
I can't walk as fast as I like
Or do anything too heavy~darn it.
Still have Morley's Choc's & coffee--

I was teasing when I called you crybaby.

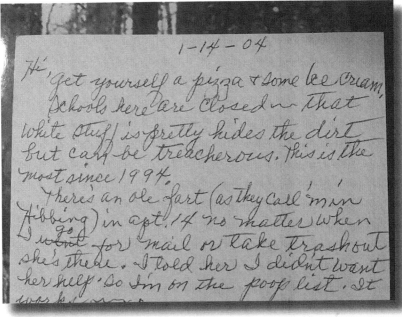

"Get yourself a pizza & some ice cream..."

KIM SUHR is the author of *Maybe I'll Learn: Snapshots of a Novice Mom* and Director of Red Oak Writing. Her fiction has recently appeared at *Midwest Review, Stonecoast Review, Solstice Literary Magazine,* and others. In addition, her work has been recognized in Wisconsin Writers Association contests. Kim holds an MFA from the Solstice Program at Pine Manor College in Boston where she was the Dennis Lehane Fellow in 2013. To learn more about Kim's writing, please visit kimsuhr.com.

This piece was inspired by a photo in the attic of my childhood home. It depicted a dark-haired girl, maybe thirteen years of age, in repose surrounded by flowers and in a white-lined casket. The photograph captivated and haunted me, and I couldn't resist hefting myself through the hole-in-the-ceiling portal into the stuffy attic to study it. I was told the photograph was probably taken because there had been no others of the girl while she was alive and that photos like this were not so unusual.

I didn't realize it then, but I'm sure I was troubled (still am) by the out-of-order circumstance of a girl dying before she had the chance to have a "living" picture taken, how wrong it is for a child to leave this world before her parents do. I couldn't (still can't) ignore what the picture revealed about my own mortality.

I wrote this piece of microfiction thinking about my friend who was undergoing chemotherapy. I couldn't imagine how difficult it must have been to tell her mother about the diagnosis and how much I would want to protect my own mother under the same circumstances. How would I tell her? I hope never to find out.

BY KIM SUHR

Wind the Fabric Tighter

AZURE INFINITY SCARF hides my chemo port, as I pull the pen across a hungry page. I write of visits to a stifling attic forty summers past, when — very much alive — I studied sepia people, long dead. Stern Germans, slight Bohemians, the girl in a casket with a halo of flowers, her posthumous portrait the only proof she'd lived.

Needing to know her, wanting to feel her, I made a casket of an old trunk, cloaked it in faded silk flowers, bribed my brother to photograph me as I lay, arms folded, eyes closed, in death.

When the print came back, Mother shrieked, "What were you thinking?!?" Tore it to pieces, threw it in the trash. She must not have known about the girl in the attic. She must not know about me.

As my pen scratches paper, I remind myself of the miles I have walked, the poems I have written, the loves I have known — so many more than the girl. Then, I see Mother, her neck in ropes as she tore the picture. I lay down my pen and wind the fabric tighter.

Australian writer **JULIE ANNE THORNDYKE** graduated with merit from the Master of Creative Writing program at the University of Sydney. She has published poems and stories for adults and children in many literary journals. She facilitates a tanka-writers group, participates in collaborative poetry presentations, and leads creative writing workshops.

Two collections of her tanka poetry are available from Ginninderra Press. In 2017, Julie was appointed editor of *Eucalypt: a tanka journal*. Read more of her work at jthorndyke.wordpress.com.

When I was a child, it was part of our family folklore that Auntie Myrtle had "a flair for writing." Apart from her dates of birth and death (1890–1970), this, and the memorable visit from her teacher to the family home to plead her case, are the main facts of her life as recorded in family history. She never married but dedicated her life to church and family. That I never saw any of her written work was mysterious.

Sensing an untold story, I began to trawl available historical sources: the family history book collated by a distant cousin; old photographs; the wonderful online resource from the National Library of Australia, Trove. Trove contains digital archives of local newspapers that give detailed accounts of weddings, social events, and church gatherings of even ordinary Australians, such as my great-grandparents.

By searching Trove, I discovered a poem that I believe was written by my great aunt, Violet Myrtle Becker. Both the name mentioned and date of publication correlate with recorded events, and the sentimental lines help to color the black-and-white sketch we have of Myrtle's life. There is more to discover — or recreate — and I hope that my relatives will be happy with my joining of the the dotted lines in writing this fictive version of our aunt's story.

BY JULIE ANNE THORNDYKE

Aunt Becker's Secret

"Woodpark," Smithfield, 1900

There's a lull in the late afternoon. Susannah has dealt with the cooking of the day; the evening meal is organized and waits for finishing when the sun goes down. She brings William a cup of tea on the front verandah: they sit, sandstone flags glowing in the afternoon light. A buttered drop-scone to keep him going until meal time. Despite Susannah's good food, he is still as wiry as ever: times are harder and he can't afford to pay hired hands, so he works the market garden himself with their elder boys. The babies are playing on a tartan blanket spread on the flags. Susannah is watchful of the bees buzzing around the flowers in her cottage garden and whisks them away with a flick of her apron. She feeds pieces of scone to the toddler who climbs onto her lap. She believes a child should carry a little extra chubbiness — a reserve in case of illness — and with eleven healthy children living out of twelve births, who is to say she is wrong?

The older children, swinging satchels, casting off hats, pinafore strings untied and flying, rush through the gate and kiss the babies.

"I know a secret, I know a secret," chants eight-year-old Ivy.

"You don't know nothin," says her brother Harold.

Susannah sends them round the back to wash and find scones waiting for them on the kitchen table.

"Pa! Ma!" says Violet Myrtle, ten years old and all of a flush. "Mr. Miller gave me one hundred percent! First of all the class..."

"That's a reason to celebrate," cries William, who jumps up and waltzes the girl around the gravel path. He hums as they dance, ending with a curtsey and a wave of his battered hat. "Time to collect the eggs, my young scholar," he says.

"I will! I'll do it," Violet declares. William goes to check the barns. "I'm going to be a teacher one day," she confides to her mother, then runs off to gather eggs.

Susannah leans back in her wicker chair, gazes at the sky turning mauve and tangerine. A teacher? Not if William has anything to do with it: he firmly holds that a woman's only place is in the home. But who knows? Perhaps for Violet he will soften. She is so like him: she has the same driven intensity, the same singleness of purpose. There is electric light in Sydney town, a telephone exchange and all manner of new things...who can tell what may happen?

❖ ❖ ❖

"Woodpark," Smithfield, 1904

It was drizzling from a grey sky as Mr. Miller walked the long miles to Woodpark Rd. For more than twenty years he had been teaching at Smithfield Public School, but he had never visited the Becker home. Rain burnt off into humidity as he walked the rutted dirt roads, rougher and less maintained the farther west he walked from Parramatta. An Anglican, he had not been part of the Wesleyan church gatherings that the Beckers attended. He knew the family mainly through the children who were students in his school, and by reputation: the mother's legendary baking, the Teutonic father's authoritarian style.

As Mr. Miller approached the Becker property, the sun was blazing through his tweed coat, and his bunions were causing discomfort inside his Sunday boots. The shine he had polished up before leaving home ten miles ago was long dusted over. From the road he had a good view of the orderly rows of cabbages, the military precision of staked tomato plants, irrigation dams and gravel paths neatly formed.

Outbuildings in good repair. A profusion of roses, nasturtiums and day lilies tumbled around the path to the house. He opened the gate, closing it gently after him, wincing at the squeak of the hinge. His feet crunched the gravel as he walked, suddenly reticent, to the shade of the verandah and the closed front door. It was a house like many others in the district: plain timber verandah posts wreathed with wisteria, two paned windows either side of a paneled cedar door. Chairs and potted plants on the sandstone floor protected by a sloping iron roof. Walls, not of timber, brick, or stone...some kind of plaster rendering? He saw a movement behind a lace curtain on the window to the left.

He knocked.

And waited.

A full ten minutes, by the pocket watch chained to his waistcoat. He pulled a monogrammed handkerchief from his pocket and dried sweat from his neck. His shirt was damp beneath his waistcoat and tie. He removed his felt hat, reshaped the brim.

At last the door opened. The eldest Miss Becker (whom he had never taught since she had been past fourteen, school leaving age, on their arrival to the district) invited him into the parlor: there was no hallway. Susannah Becker rose from her chair to greet him.

"Pardon the unwanted intrusion, Mrs. Becker," he said. "I apologize for arriving with no invitation. I do hope that Mr. Becker may be at home?"

William Becker was out the back, washing mud from his hands, tidying himself into the fresh clothes that his wife had thrust at him before taking her place, hair tidied and apron removed, in the parlor.

"Yes, indeed he is!" Susannah was all smiles. "Lizzie, fetch your father. Then please bring us some tea — if you will, Mr. Miller? Or lemonade? We can all be comfortable with some refreshments."

Lizzie did as she was bid. With help from her five sisters, who were lurking quietly in the kitchen, she prepared tea and set out food on the best china. Ivy put fresh scones on a plate with a cut-glass bowl of jam. Myrtle made triangular watercress sandwiches. Lizzie laid the round cedar table in the parlor with a white-embroidered linen cloth, silver sugar tongs, and her mother's good cups and saucers. The other girls stayed out of the way in the kitchen. The boys were nowhere to be seen.

Mr. Miller sat on a balloon-backed chair and enquired after Susannah's health.

William came in, hair wetly flat on his head, fresh shirt buttoned to his chin and neatly tucked into trousers supported by braces. He hadn't bothered with coat, collar, or tie. The men shook hands. Mr. Miller praised the rows of cabbages, enquired about market prices, lamented the lack of good rain.

"We are fortunate to have the canal running behind our land," William replied.

"The canal from Prospect Reservoir?" Mr. Miller asked.

"Yes, Prospect canal runs along behind," William said. "So we have water free for the taking at any time of year."

"Very canny of you to choose such a spot, Mr. Becker," replied Mr. Miller. "And you have been here in Smithfield for...ten years?"

"Not quite ten," Susannah replied. "Although William came out first with the eldest boy, to build the house, while I stayed with the children in Botany."

"Botany Bay?"

"Yes. My family still live in St. Peters and Botany. Our market garden there...was much larger than this. William employed many Chinamen...but the land there, too expensive now...and the smell of factories and the noise..."

"We are happy in Smithfield," said William. "Good air to breathe and space to live."

"Pardon me, Mr. Becker, for asking... you built the house yourself?"

"Built it from the clay of the land. It is a pisé house."

"A very fine building, Mr. Becker. An excellent solution."

Lizzie brought ginger cake: Susannah poured tea. She asked Mr. Miller about the academic progress of her school-age children. With six of the eleven attending Mr. Miller's school, this took some time. If there had been any rustlings coming from the kitchen, now they ceased.

He saved Violet Myrtle for last.

"She is a scholar, Mrs Becker. A scholar to her bones and a writer of talent. Of potential. If you and Mr. Becker could see your way clear..."

"A girl's place is in the home," said William. "Helping her mother."

"For some girls, yes, this is the right thing," agreed Mr. Miller. "But for Violet..."

"She must learn her duty."

"Mr. Becker, you were born in a country of artists, philosophers — of scholars and teachers — you must recognize in your daughter the talents God has given..."

"Gott requires us to be as he has made us. To work, to respect our Mutter and our Vater, to praise our Maker," said William.

Susannah offered more tea. When William's carefully Anglicized speech slipped back into the German accents of his childhood, emotions were on the rise.

Mr. Miller took from his breast pocket a folded paper. "This...is a poem written by Violet Myrtle. An extraordinary thing for a girl her age to have written — can you not see? An exception must be made for her..."

William shook his head, and inspected his boots.

Mr. Miller was not ready to concede. "Mrs. Becker. There are scholarships. To the Sydney Girls High School. You have relatives nearer to the school, where Violet could board, yes? Or the Wesleyan Ladies College. She could travel by train there as a day student. There are ways of bringing this about."

"Could she not continue with you at Smithfield school?" suggested Susannah.

"We have asked, and asked, as you well know," Mr. Miller said, shaking his head, "for a higher class to be added, also for a high school...but because we have a railway station, the department says those students wishing for further study must travel to other schools."

"No." William was on his feet. "Mr. Miller, we appreciate your kindness. We appreciate your interest in our children. But my daughters do not go out into the world like men. This is the way Gott wills it."

"Another piece of cake?" asked Susannah. "You had a long walk, Mr. Miller."

"You walked, Mr Miller?" asked William. "From Parramatta?"

"Yes."

"I'll carry you back in the sulky. I have some business in town."

Mr Miller rose to look his host in the eye. "No need, Mr. Becker."

"No need, as you have the feet that Gott gave you with which to walk, but I also have the horse and sulky with which Gott has blessed me. So I will be glad to share this gift with you and welcome."

"...and Violet Myrtle's gifts..." The teacher stretched out both hands in entreaty.

The clock on the mantelpiece ticked with a slow, solemn beat. Susannah twisted the white linen handkerchief in tense hands. William adjusted his braces and straightened his work-worn shoulders. "Violet will use her gifts as Gott wants. In church, at home, in her family. As Gott wills."

In the kitchen, the sound of breaking crockery.

❖ ❖ ❖

Smithfield, 1910

Violet Myrtle always had letters to post. Letters to collect. Her boots tramped to the post office as if they knew the way without any direction from her mind. This was a good thing, because she had the writerly habit of observing: the colors of the sky, the grasses bent by the north wind, the wombat lumbering into his burrow. Often a snatch of hymn would be on her lips as she walked: "All things praise thee — Lord, may we!"

Myrtle wrote to members of her family, those brothers and sisters now married and living around the country. To school friends gone out into the world; to pen-friends gleaned from magazines. She wrote to church missionaries needing news from home and godly encouragement. She also wrote to her much-loved former teacher, Mr. Miller. He had retired the year after Myrtle left school, and moved away. He wrote, encouraging her poetry efforts, helping her polish and correct her verses as he had in school, advising on meter and rhyme. Her poems were hymn-like: little wonder! Every Sunday twice at the Methodist church, come rain or shine. Conventional, yet sincere, verses of sentimental subjects.

It was Mr. Miller who had sent the first poem to a newspaper. Not under her real name: not quite. There had been such a fuss when, at age eight, younger sister Ivy had written a limerick at school which had been entered in a competition, submitted as a batch by Mr. Miller to the local rag. Ivy had won a cash prize and the limerick was published with her name. Father was not pleased.

No, definitely not safe to publish under Violet Myrtle's real name until she was twenty-one and allowed some freedom. That first poem, and the many that followed, were published under the name of Charlotte Becker. A little nod to Charlotte Brontë, who had also famously used a non de plume. Father never knew. Myrtle, Ivy, or another of the sisters, who had been let into the secret (sharing a bedroom, all six of them, until they left to be married—how could they not know?) always collected mail. Myrtle's many letters—there were always some with foreign stamps from missionaries, pen-friends—made it easy for a few from editors near and far to be hidden in the midst of the pile.

In her roll-top desk, she kept the editors' letters hidden away. The checks were another matter—she was earning money from her verse! What to do? A bank account would be evidence, hard to conceal from father. To soothe her conscience, to mitigate against her deceit, she donated all her fees to the missionary fund. The exception she made was at Christmas, when she cashed a large check in Parramatta and bought gifts for the family.

Although William's daughters were not allowed to take jobs, to help family members was perfectly alright. As Myrtle's older siblings married and raised children, she was able to visit them, helping with their domestic arrangements, nursing children if sick, helping a sister expecting a blessed event. Sadly, sometimes both coincided.

The second eldest daughter, Alice, married a local boy, Charles Coleman, in 1908. There were almost as many Colemans in the local school as Beckers. In 1910, the twenty-year-old Myrtle went to stay with them to help Alice, who was ill and expecting her second child. The first, Elsie, was a favorite with Myrtle. Eighteen months old, a sweet little girl of placid temperament, she was a delight to care for. Diphtheria struck. Myrtle nursed both the child and the mother. Charles was in despair. Another Becker sister, Lilian, came to help. The doctor visited daily. But a sad little coffin was carried from the house to the graveyard next to the Smithfield church, despite everyone's prayers. Elsie was lost to them. Lilian stayed to help with the new baby, a boy. Myrtle went home to grieve.

She had no other way to express her sorrow but with words: and they poured out. The poem "The Angel-Child" was sent out to a newspaper under her own name, Violet M. Becker. Close enough to twenty-one, she was willing to take on her father. There would be places of safe haven amongst her siblings' houses if he roared beyond bearing.

The Angel-Child

A little head crowned with bright curling hair
Once graced my home;
Its owner now in Heaven is gathered safe,
No more to roam.

A fair young brow to which my loving lips
Were oft times pressed,
Free from care, now calmly leans upon
The Father's breast.

Dark, thoughtful eyes were wont to seek my own
With glances bright;
Now they behold the Saviour on His Throne
In realms of light.

Two sweet red lips, whose sunny smiles of yore
My heart did cheer,
Chant hymns of praise to Him who gently dries
Her every tear.

Soft little hand, once tightly clamped in mine
No more I hold;
The Shepherd came and led my wee lamb home
To His own fold.

Two tiny feet whose pattering steps I heard
In days of old,
Now tread, untired, the bright Celestial streets
All paved with gold.

How lone is earth, bereft of Elsie's voice,
Her presence sweet,
Her loving smiles, her soft endearing ways,
Her pattering feet.

How bright is Heaven! For there my loved one dwells,
And there she waits
To welcome me, when I at length shall reach
The pearly gates.

Oh blessed day! When we again shall meet
To part no more!
Ended all grief, all loneliness and pain —
Our sorrows o'er.

- Violet M. Becker

Guildford, 1970

Ivy looked around the crowded room her sister Myrtle had crammed with books. Squeezed into it, too, were the iron-framed tester beds of their girlhood, the cedar drawers and washstand, the roll-top desk at which Myrtle had scribbled night and day. Gone now, Violet Myrtle Becker had left behind a house full of mementos and no descendants.

"Mum, what about these oil lamps?" asked Alison. The only unmarried one of Ivy's eight children, Alison had taken leave-of-absence to help sort out Auntie Myrtle's estate. A teacher, she had also become a headmistress, and at fifty was a government administrator.

"We'll keep those," Ivy replied. Her neat and tidy home was suddenly augmented by antiques. The oil lamps. A glass dome on a timber base to hold specimen flowers. Many books. Together they sorted rubbish, sold the antique furniture and gave smaller items to extended family members as keepsakes. There were many cupboards full of old linen and piles of papers to sort. Bundles tied with string. Letters, empty envelopes, handwritten drafts, published stories in Sunday School magazines. Boxes of poems by someone called Charlotte Becker — letters from editors to this Charlotte at the old Woodpark address.

As Alison worked through her aunt's correspondence, as far back as the letters from Mr. Miller, she began to piece together Myrtle's secret literary life. This strict and religious old maid, with her devout stories and didactic poems, the author of a militaristic temperance hymn of the 1920s,* had also written of love, passion, and loss. Alison had been encouraged by her aunt to become a teacher, and knew that it had been Myrtle's own dream. That it had been denied her. Now, the evidence suggested that Myrtle had found other ways for her creativity to thrive.

❖ ❖ ❖

---

* *Methodist* (Sydney, NSW : 1892 - 1954), Saturday 9 January 1926, page 6 National Library of Australia http://nla.gov.au/nla.news-article155358287. THERE'S A FOE THAT WOULD CONQUER AUSTRALIA — V. M. Becker

I must enter this story now.

Ivy, my grandmother, having kept the secret for sixty years, told her daughter Alison, my aunt, about Myrtle's non-de plume. Then she quietly took the documents home. Whatever Grandma did with them, I never knew. I never saw any of Great Auntie Myrtle's writing as a child. It was through her collection of books that I knew her.

It became a Sunday ritual for me to return and borrow a cloth-bound, sentimental Victorian novel, one at a time, from the makeshift shelves in Grandma's garage. Auntie Alison was sometimes there when I visited my grandmother each week. At ten years old, I was in awe of my taciturn teacher aunt. I was a silent listener to the adult conversations about wills and funerals.

One Sunday, arriving at Grandma's house, the ten-year-old me went to return the novel I had borrowed. All Great Auntie Myrtle's books were gone. A second-hand book dealer had come and taken the lot. I was heart-broken. I still have that borrowed novel. Grandma knew more than she let on. I was only ten, but she saved for me one other book of poetry, inscribed on the foxed fly-leaf to "Wood-Violet" — her sister who was not allowed to become a teacher, but who quietly found her own purpose in the world.

❖ ❖ ❖

Today, I trawl digitized newspapers and magazines for the poems Aunt Becker published. Did she really use the name Charlotte Becker? Am I on the right track? I don't know for sure. Alison and Grandma are both gone now: there is no one to ask. My imagination works overtime, as I compare poems by writers in the old newspapers and archives. The story of my resilient Aunt Becker fascinates me.

I was a child when she died, and my memories of her are few. A thin, angular woman with long, straight dark hair, that if loosed from her hairnet and unwound, was long enough to sit on. Small, dark but shining, alert eyes that looked keenly into a child's face, into my face. Perhaps my fascination with her story comes from the memory of those eyes and their piercing gaze, daring me to be myself, daring me to surmount all obstacles and be the writer she recognized in the bookish child she saw before her.

About the Editors

CHRISTI CRAIG works as a sign language interpreter by day and moonlights as a writer, teacher, and editor. She teaches online courses that focus on story structure, creativity, and flash nonfiction. She is also a volunteer instructor for the Creative Writing Class at Harwood Place Retirement Living Center in Wauwatosa, Wisconsin, where she has edited four anthologies of poems, stories, and essays.

Christi was an Assistant Editor at *Compose* Literary Journal and an Associate Editor for *Noble / Gas Quarterly*. She also volunteered on the novel acquisitions team during the 2016 submissions call for Forest Avenue Press. Her own stories and essays have appeared online and in print, and she received an Honorable Mention in *Glimmer Train*'s Family Matters Competition, 2010. Visit her website at christicraig.com for more information about her classes, editing, and published works.

LISA RIVERO is a writer, book indexer, and the publisher of Hidden Timber Books in Milwaukee, Wisconsin. She enjoys writing fiction, poetry, and non-fiction. Some of her publications include a food and wellness column, magazine and journal articles, four non-fiction books, a middle-grade historical novel, and a blog at *Psychology Today*.

Lisa has a master's degree in Literary Studies from the University of Wisconsin-Milwaukee, and she taught college-level writing and creative thinking courses for many years before making the transition to full-time writing and publishing. She has been a keynote speaker and workshop presenter at both national and regional conferences, and her professional interests include creativity, literature and the humanities, and the challenges faced by writers and others in this fast-paced and often perplexing twenty-first century. Visit lisarivero.com to learn more about her writing career and speaking topics. For more information about Hidden Timber Books, go to hiddentimberbooks.com.

Made in the USA
Middletown, DE
28 May 2017